KING RULES

KING RULES

TEN TRUTHS FOR YOU, YOUR FAMILY, AND OUR NATION TO PROSPER

ALVEDA KING

NELSON
BOOKS

An Imprint of Thomas Nelson

Published in Nashville, Tennessee, by Nelson Books, an imprint of Thomas Nelson. Nelson Books and Thomas Nelson are registered trademarks of HarperCollins Christian Publishing, Inc.

Thomas Nelson, Inc., titles may be purchased in bulk for educational, business, fund-raising, or sales promotional use. For information, please e-mail SpecialMarkets@ThomasNelson.com.

Scripture quotations marked ESV are from THE ENGLISH STANDARD VERSION. © 2001 by Crossway Bibles, a division of Good News Publishers.

Scripture quotations marked NKJV are from THE NEW KING JAMES VERSION. © 1982 by Thomas Nelson, Inc. Used by permission. All rights reserved.

Scripture quotations marked KJV are from the King James Version, which is in the public domain.

Scripture marked DRB are from the Douay-Rheims Bible, which is in the public domain.

Scripture quotations marked NASB are from NEW AMERICAN STANDARD BIBLE®. © The Lockman Foundation 1960, 1962, 1963, 1968, 1971, 1972, 1973, 1975, 1977, 1995. Used by permission.

Scripture quotations marked NIV are from the Holy Bible, New International Version˚, NIV˚. © 1973, 1978, 1984, 2011 by Biblica, Inc.™ Used by permission of Zondervan. All rights reserved worldwide. www.zondervan.com

Scripture quotations marked NLT are from *Holy Bible*, New Living Translation. © 1996, 2004, 2007. Used by permission of Tyndale House Publishers, Inc., Wheaton, Illinois 60189. All rights reserved.

Scripture quotations marked YLT are from Young's Literal Translation, which is in the public domain.

Dorothy Law Nolte's poem, "Children Learn What They Live" on page 61, copyright © 1972/1975 by Dorothy Law Nolte. Author-approved short version. Used by permission.

ISBN: 9781400205004

Library of Congress Control Number: 2014931447

Printed in the United States of America

14 15 16 17 RRD 6 5 4 3 2 1

May the king's rule be refreshing like spring rain on freshly cut grass, like the showers that water the earth.

Psalm 72:6 NLT

Contents

Foreword by the Hon. J. C. Watts ix

Introduction xiii

The Family Tree .xvi

A Word About Names xix

RULE NO. 1
MAKE HOME A PRIORITY 1

RULE NO. 2
SERVE YOUR FAMILY 23

RULE NO. 3
GET A GOOD EDUCATION 43

CONTENTS

RULE NO. 4

GUARD YOUR HEART 63

RULE NO. 5

DEFEND LIFE 83

RULE NO. 6

FIGHT FOR JUSTICE 101

RULE NO. 7

CARE FOR THE NEEDY 119

RULE NO. 8

WORK FOR PEACE 131

RULE NO. 9

BUILD THE BELOVED COMMUNITY 155

RULE NO. 10

FIND YOUR JOY 167

If Uncle M.L. Could Tweet 181

Afterword by Father Frank Pavone 187

Sources 191

Acknowledgments 195

About the Author 197

FOREWORD

I f you listen to the media today—which is almost unavoidable—you'll hear about the problems besetting our nation and our culture. Chances are you'll hear some politician or self-appointed spokesperson saying that whatever the problem is, it's being caused by someone else. And that someone else will then be demonized while the problem fades into the background, only to be replaced by the next crisis to be used as a bludgeon against another political opponent.

"The politics of personal destruction"—a phrase popularized by President Bill Clinton during his impeachment and a tactic probably as old as man's fallen nature—are alive and well. Having been on the front line of politics, I have been the target of entrenched leaders who would rather hurl epithets than try to defend their indefensible positions. It happened when I was a congressman; it happens now.

Those who have been the overseers of the black family's destruction and, increasingly, the demise of families of all colors, are more protective of their power than they are zealous for solutions, so they attack anyone who dares to point out the obvious—that their programs aren't working.

Officials who have busted the national budget just don't want to hear that we're running out of money, so they malign anyone with an adding machine. They want us to buy into the myth that $2 + 2 = 6$, and when anyone says that $2 + 2 = 4$, they are labeled extreme or radical.

Too many of our leaders, when confronted with the results of their actions, respond by pointing and saying, "He did them!"

To put it bluntly, integrity, responsibility, and moral courage seem to be in short supply today. But where can we find them?

Alveda King knows where to look. Alveda and her family, like so many of us and our families, have *been there*. She was raised amid turmoil in an unfair society that treated her as not good enough. Her family came from sharecroppers. They never stopped working and never stopped learning. Each generation built on the foundation of its predecessors.

Unlike most of us, Alveda knew death and terror at a young age. She knew violence and loss. She knew all this because her family stood for values and beliefs that throughout history have shaken established orders and set the captives free—values and beliefs that built our nation and can set us back on course.

King Rules offers bedrock values that have been handed down, not coincidentally, through a long line of preachers. They are character-building, practical beliefs that transcend and overcome circumstance. They taught generations of King men and women. They taught my family. In years gone by they taught most Americans. If our nation is to prosper, they must inform us again so our children's families will carry them forward.

These King Rules endure because they are, at their essence, the values of the King, our Savior Jesus Christ. They are timeless because while eras and places change, human nature does not. History shows that as hatred, cruelty, greed, and selfishness keep reappearing, they must be met with the radical truths that love is what is commanded of us, and justice is what we must seek.

These basic truths are what motivated the Reverend Martin Luther King Jr. when he was spat upon, threatened, and jailed. He did not persevere through persecution to achieve political or personal gain; he did so because he was taught to love his neighbor with a love that manifests itself in service and sacrifice. Rev. King's love was not just intellectual; he lived it. His love for others still endures, inspires, and changes lives. It's a love that doesn't make you perfect in this life, but makes you want to be.

King Rules is a firsthand account of one of the most important periods in our nation's history, but it's also a treasure of wisdom gleaned from hard lessons, simple truths, and loving parents. It's more than Alveda's story; it's an account of the beliefs that redirected the course of a nation, left us a legacy, and hopefully will guide us again.

Hon. J. C. Watts

Introduction

Another milestone was reached as I finished this book. The fiftienth anniversary of Uncle M.L.'s "I Have a Dream" speech and the historic March on Washington was just behind us, and the fiftieth anniversary of the 1964 civil rights act was just ahead. This season allowed me and the world to ask, "Is the dream now fulfilled?" Though I remain unable to say that the dream of Dr. Martin Luther King Jr. has been fulfilled, I do know that we have made some progress.

Understanding there is so much more required to realize the fullness of the dream, I am encouraged to look back while moving forward. The lessons, the rules as it were, that were learned from my ancestors remain a beacon of hope and light for me and prayerfully for you as well. There are still many questions and many miles to go. And yet I do believe that we will reach that promised land.

Among the many questions people often ask regarding Dr. Martin Luther King Jr. and what it has been like growing up in his family, I am most honored when people ask things like: Did you really know him? Where did he get his strength and power?

In *King Rules* you will find the answers to these questions and so much more. But this is not just another book about Dr. Martin Luther King Jr. There are many good and noble accounts about his life. There are also his own books. I hope this little book about his family and our values will bring insight and enlightenment about the background and foundations that nurtured and fostered the man Martin, who has been either honored or hated by the masses and dearly loved by his natural family.

I want to share the rules that allowed our family to prosper. I firmly believe they will help your family—and our nation—prosper as well.

As I was compiling notes for this book, I was tempted to shy away from controversial topics like human sexuality and abortion and stick to safe topics like education, peace, poverty, and the like. After all, people sometimes don't want to hear viewpoints that are not on the same page as their philosophy of choice. Yet I had to remember that my uncle M.L. and other family members often trod the road less traveled and were not afraid to speak truth, even when the topics were controversial.

Uncle M.L. said once that it's not where we stand in moments of comfort that count, but where we stand in times of controversy that will be remembered. Since members of our family have had close encounters with some of the more controversial issues, it seems fitting to include lessons learned on the journey to truth regarding even the most painful of them.

Martin Luther King Jr. didn't grow up in a vacuum, and he is survived by relatives: the Kings and the Williamses. So I've included a Williams–King family tree depicting ancestors and descendants.

Finally, please remember that inside these pages are recollections of principles, lessons, and truths that I learned from my uncle and other members of my family. With the eyes of the world on us, we in the Williams–King family have lived through pain and yet have not lost our joy.

We wish to share our experiences with you. Please get to know us as a human family, people who have loved and served our Creator, and who have given our all for the human family the Creator loves so very much. May this journal bring you much peace and prosperity in your soul and prosperity on your life's journey.

SEVEN GENERATIONS OF WILLIAMS/KING FAMILY LEGACY

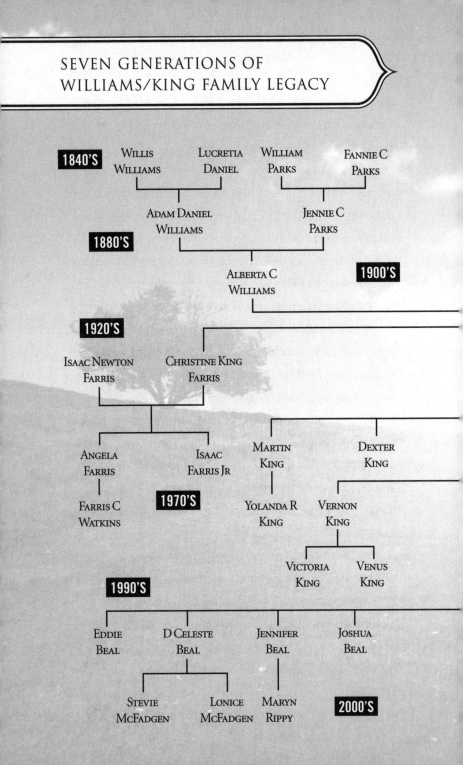

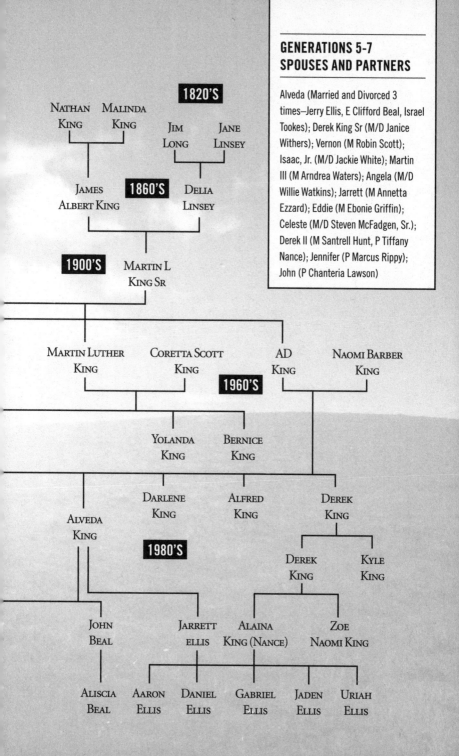

GENERATIONS 5-7 SPOUSES AND PARTNERS

Alveda (Married and Divorced 3 times—Jerry Ellis, E Clifford Beal, Israel Tookes); Derek King Sr (M/D Janice Withers); Vernon (M Robin Scott); Isaac, Jr. (M/D Jackie White); Martin III (M Arndrea Waters); Angela (M/D Willie Watkins); Jarrett (M Annetta Ezzard); Eddie (M Ebonie Griffin); Celeste (M/D Steven McFadgen, Sr.); Derek II (M Santrell Hunt, P Tiffany Nance); Jennifer (P Marcus Rippy); John (P Chanteria Lawson)

1820'S

NATHAN KING   MALINDA KING   JIM LONG   JANE LINSEY

JAMES ALBERT KING   1860'S   DELIA LINSEY

1900'S   MARTIN L KING SR

MARTIN LUTHER KING   CORETTA SCOTT KING   1960'S   AD KING   NAOMI BARBER KING

YOLANDA KING   BERNICE KING

ALVEDA KING   DARLENE KING   ALFRED KING   DEREK KING

1980'S

DEREK KING   KYLE KING

JOHN BEAL   JARRETT ELLIS   ALAINA KING (NANCE)   ZOE NAOMI KING

ALISCIA BEAL   AARON ELLIS   DANIEL ELLIS   GABRIEL ELLIS   JADEN ELLIS   URIAH ELLIS

A Word About Names

E very family has familiar names it uses for its members, pet names, nicknames, and the like. You'll find a few of those here, so I thought I'd give you a list so you can keep track of exactly who's who.

MARTIN LUTHER KING JR. is how most people know my uncle—MLK for short. I mostly call him Uncle M.L.

ALFRED DANIEL KING was Uncle M.L.'s brother. He went by A.D. King, but I mostly call him Daddy because that's who he was to me. Not to be confused with Daddy King.

DADDY KING was my paternal granddaddy. I call him Daddy King and Granddaddy in the book.

His given name was Michael Luther King, and people often called him Big Mike. Later in life he took the name Martin. There's a story to that, but you'll have to keep reading to find out more.

BIG MAMA was my paternal grandmother. Her legal name was Alberta Williams King after Daddy King married her, but Granddaddy always called her Honey Bunch.

NAOMI BARBER was my mom. Her nickname in the family was Neenie.

BIG MAMA BESSIE was my maternal grandmother.

ADAM DANIEL WILLIAMS was Great-granddaddy to me, and that's what I call him here.

RULE NO. 1

Make Home a Priority

W hen people come to visit me in Atlanta, one of my favorite things is to take them to see the historic King family home at 501 Auburn Avenue, the home where my father, uncle, and aunt were born. The house, built in 1895, is now part of the Martin Luther King Jr. National Historic Site. But it is also the house where my parents were living when I was born. And it's the house where my grandmother, Alberta Williams King, lived when she was a child.

Sometimes, as a special gift, I do private civil rights tours for people. I always take them to visit the "Birth Home." It resonates in some way with everyone. I think that is because it so strongly represents what home meant and still means to the King family.

My great-granddaddy, Adam Daniel Williams, bought the home with his young wife, Jenny Celeste Parks, a few years after moving to Atlanta and becoming pastor of Ebenezer Baptist Church. It was a large Queen Anne–style home a block and a half south of the church. Can you imagine how he felt? Great-granddaddy was born into slavery, but here he was the pastor of a growing congregation, living in a beautiful home with his beloved wife and a new baby daughter— Alberta Christine, my grandmamma. I always knew her as Big Mama.

Great-granddaddy and Jenny opened their doors to the people of their congregation, the community, traveling missionaries, and others during those days when blacks were not allowed to rest in the segregated hotels and establishments. Big Mike King was one of the men who came around back then. He walked from Stockbridge, Georgia, to Atlanta with his shoes slung over his back because he didn't want to wear holes in his only pair. He knew Atlanta would help him realize his dream of making a difference in the world, but the city didn't welcome anyone with the smell of the farm sticking to him. The city slickers poked fun at him and said he "wore the stench of the mule." So as soon as he was able to set some money aside, Big Mike bought plenty of soap and good-smelling lotion, promising himself that his peers would never laugh at his body odor again.

It must have worked. While Big Mike worked with Great-granddaddy in the ministry, he caught young Alberta's eye. They married in 1926 and started their own family—which is how I eventually came to know Big Mike as Daddy King, my granddaddy.

When Great-granddaddy Williams died in 1931, the Williams family home became the Williams–King family home. Great-grandmother Jenny and her widowed sister, Ida, lived there, and the home was cherished and regarded as a haven for the family and anyone else in times of need.

It was there that Aunt Christine, Uncle M.L., and Daddy A.D. King were born. It was in that home that they all learned the King Rules.

❧

The parlor is the first room you see when you enter the house from the street, and the most notable thing is the Victrola and the piano. These pieces remind me of the music that has always filled our lives, wherever we lived. A home without music lacks a certain spirit. Whether classical, gospel, jazz, or pop music, it affects our souls. Any kind of music with strong healing qualities can soothe dark moods, uplift spirits, and create a soundtrack of joy and tranquility.

Singing plays an important role in the King legacy. My mother Naomi, Aunt Coretta, and Aunt Christine were concert soloists during their earlier days. Their voices helped to raise funds for the civil rights movement, because there were fund-raising concerts in churches and meeting halls back then.

Of course, there are the musicians also. My daddy played the violin, and they all played a bit of piano. Big Mama was a noted concert pianist, my sister Darlene had a beautiful touch on the keys, and several of my children are either singers or musicians. I'm known to sing and play a bit as well.

Not that everyone was always happy about learning to play. The truth is that Daddy and Uncle M.L. hated piano lessons. They disliked the experience so much they resorted to extreme measures. One time the piano teacher—by all accounts a stern instructor who rapped their knuckles if they made a mistake—arrived at the house to discover that the legs on the piano stool had been sawn off. My daddy and uncle were planning for "a fall from grace" to bring an end to their excruciating lessons. Another time Daddy and Uncle M.L. took to the keys with a hammer to make the instrument impossible to play. As a minister Granddaddy believed in the Bible. I'm sure you've heard, "Spare the rod and spoil the child." I believe that Daddy and Uncle M.L. felt the power of that verse that day.

Daddy and M.L. were unrepentant pranksters who found every opportunity they could to pull one of their good-natured tricks. Sometimes Aunt Christine joined in the fun. The three of them would borrow Grandma Jenny's fox fur stole. The wrap was so authentic it still had the heads of three little foxes attached. Aunt Chris, Uncle M.L., and Daddy would put the stole on a stick and poke it through the hedges in the front yard to scare passersby. One man was so frightened he went running down the street so fast that his fancy Sunday hat flew off in the wind.

For those who believe that Dr. Martin Luther King Jr. emerged from Big Mama's womb as a paragon of perfection, I hope this reality check isn't too traumatic for your sensibilities. But Uncle M.L. was a normal little boy, and he and his brother engaged in childish pursuits.

When she wasn't helping them get in trouble, Aunt Christine was always there to remind them of their upbringing. And when things became too exciting, their parents were there with loving discipline and guidance.

They were being prepared for leadership, allowed to develop their personalities in preparation to yield those very individual personalities over to a Higher Purpose.

❧

This speaks to me about a very different aspect of a home—it needs to be a place where all members of the household can express themselves. It's important that every voice be heard. When parents take time to listen, they can hear the errors, which is important. They can also hear evidence of the unique traits that need to be cultivated in their child, which is even more important. In both cases it's essential that parents have the final say in using God's Word while teaching children the way they should go.

This might be one of the most significant lessons about the tradition of home we have in the King family. From the time we were very young, we were encouraged to express ourselves; we learned that we could talk about anything we wanted, as long as we did so respectfully. I think this is tremendously important, because it develops healthy self-image at an early age and it teaches the value of communication. This pays back big as children get older.

I always felt that I could express myself to my parents and grandparents, especially my mother and grand-mother. One of my mother's favorite sayings was, "You can't clean house by sweeping the dirt under the rug. Bring it into the light." She meant we couldn't cleanse our souls by hiding our sins. Instead, agape love, repentance, forgiveness, and humility can fix our problems. In this spirit she made it clear I could talk to her about anything.

Because I had such an open avenue of communication with my elders, I was able to avoid many of the pitfalls in life that other children—especially teenagers—encounter. I often told them exactly what I'd been doing when I was out, and as a result received wise counsel that helped me to avoid many serious scrapes and more serious trouble. Because open communication was often the rule, many of these communication sessions took place in the family rooms of the various King households. I tend to follow this same rule today with my children and grandchildren, and it pays off.

Today the term "family room" seems to be old-fashioned. We tend to use words like "den" and "great room" instead.

Thankfully I have fond memories of our various family rooms.

In the old days the room down the hall from the parlor in the Birth Home was the family room, which also doubled as a pastor's study. This was the room where everyone would go to relax after the evening's chores were done. Family members would listen to shows on the radio or play board games. Whatever they were doing, they always put a premium on being together.

This premium family interaction is something that was passed down through every generation and remains relevant in our lives now. When I was young, the family branches often came together for big family dinners. There were holiday gatherings, weddings, and just plain wanting-to-be-together times. Sometimes we went out to restaurants, but usually we were at the homes of family members. For us these weren't traditional family reunions; they were less formal and more impromptu.

Times like these are tremendously valuable for two reasons. The first is that it exemplifies for every member of the family the importance of the family as a unit—that there's something stronger about all of us together than we can ever be as individuals. The second is that it shows each member of the family that his or her presence is cherished.

I have always found it important to send the message that in a loving family, competition is secondary. Fellowship and camaraderie come first. In our family we have had to work hard to ensure that the members are not only *loved*, but that they're *liked* as well. Sometimes we have missed the mark; but believe me, this practice becomes extremely valuable when political and emotional differences arise—and you know they do. People are people. Knowing how to love and respect each other in spite of our differences helps to keep the love alive.

~∞~

In the Birth Home there is another room where the family gathered every day, the dining room. Harmony is good for the digestion, and differences were rarely aired in that room. Instead, the dining room was a place where delicious meals for the body were served along with food for thought and development of the soul. Daddy King was absolutely adamant about having dinner together every night, even if he was working late. If he was in town, then the food didn't go down on the table until he was home.

Every dinner was preceded by one of the children

reciting a verse from the Bible, which ensured the family always understood that they first needed to praise God before partaking of His bounty. Legend has it that the children's favorite Bible verse was "Jesus wept," because it was short and reciting it assured a speedy mouthful of delicious dinner. Granddaddy was on to that little trick, though, and he insisted they learn longer verses. It would seem that this practice set the foundation for Daddy's and Uncle M.L.'s love for the Bible. It instilled the Bible in their hearts from an early age, which served Uncle M.L. and Daddy faithfully as they became men and leaders in the community.

Fellowship has always been key in the King family, and eating together helped everyone reconnect at the end of the day. The dining room provided an easy place for communication. Everyone was encouraged to speak about his or her day, which not only gave each family member a moment in the spotlight but also gave a chance to air any concerns or worries or to get advice from loved ones. The dinnertime ritual granted security to the children and communicated that they were loved and valued. It also gave the parents a chance to see how their kids were doing as they prepared their jewels to shine.

We were expected to come to the dinner table as a

family seven days a week. Daddy King instituted this requirement when his children were young, and this practice was only suspended under extreme circumstances, not on the almost daily basis that happens in so many families now. Again, this wasn't an arbitrary rule. What my family has understood for a long time is that the lines of communication are open wider when you sit down together every night. It is also invaluable for a family to see itself as a unit at least once a day. It serves as a subtle reminder of the strong bonds that unite all of us and how much bigger we are when we are all together.

This kind of family ritual has so much value. These days it might not be realistic to sit everyone down in one place every single day, especially as children get involved in school and community projects and parents take on considerable responsibilities to keep the household moving forward. But having certain days when the family always eats dinner together, or at least insisting that you do so several times a month, can be worth so, so much.

I saw the benefit of these practices growing up and tried as hard as I could to maintain them when my children were young, even as our lives sped up. Now that they are adults, some of them with children of their own, I still try to gather them together from time to time. I'm convinced there's something deeply restorative about everyone being in one place at one time as often as possible, particularly around the table.

Another place good times were had was the kitchen, down the hallway on the first floor in the back. This was everyone's favorite room in the Birth Home, and considering what great cooks Great-grandmother Jenny and Aunt Ida were, I can understand why.

Of course, Southern cooking was the order of the day back then, and fried chicken was a favorite. Staples like collard greens, fried corn, candied yams, sweet potato pie, coconut cake, and all of those "fixin's" were to be found in abundance. Other delicacies would find their way to the table. Fancy dishes of peas and salads and even wild game were not off limits. It was all usually chased down with ice-cold lemonade or tea; and in winter the family often enjoyed a mulled spiced tea blended with apple cider called Wassail.

For our family cooking has always been an essential part of the home, and we like to get everyone involved. My daddy was a gourmet cook—that's where I got my passion for it. My children are all good cooks, and even my grandchildren contribute in the kitchen. We keep them away from hot stoves and sharp knives, but they enjoy banging on pots and pans, stirring up dishes of their own, and getting involved in preparing the family meals.

To me this is an indispensable part of creating a sense of community in a household. Not only is it important that everyone eat together as often as possible, but it's also important that they create meals together when they can. When everyone gets involved with basic tasks like feeding each other, an invaluable feeling of unity develops. You can't buy that at any restaurant.

~

Granddaddy refused to have his children born in a segregated hospital. Big Mama gave birth to her three children upstairs in the master bedroom, also known as the Birth Room. It is said that when Uncle M.L., the firstborn son, was born, Granddaddy wiped away his tears of compassion shed for his wife over the long and hard delivery, let out a loud yell, and jumped high enough to touch the twelve-foot ceiling, yelling, "I have a son!"

Uncle M.L. and Daddy shared the adjoining room with their Uncle Joel, Daddy King's younger brother. Uncle Joel was there while he was completing school.

Daddy and Uncle M.L. shared the trundle. They were taught to always respect their elders and naturally understood that Uncle Joel got the larger bed. There was a tremendous amount of honor and respect for parents and all elders in the King home. This custom is still maintained in our family today.

It's a miracle Uncle Joel got any studying done in that room. By all indications it was a flurry of boys, toys, books, games, and clothes strewn about. Big Mama kept an immaculate house, but gave the boys a little leeway in their room. Daddy and my uncle always had something going on up there. It was impossible to keep everything tidy. I'm guessing Big Mama scolded them about it from time to time—but with a twinkle in her eye. She knew the messiness was a sign her sons were growing and playing and figuring out life.

Surely this is a meaningful truth to consider in all homes. The Kings have always believed that a house should be clean, but we also believe that a house should look like people actually live in it. Children should be taught to respect their things and to cherish the valuables in a house, but they shouldn't feel so restricted by rules that they can't have fun or let their imaginations soar. How else are they going to grow?

The house on Auburn Avenue was a source of great

comfort and security for my grandparents and their children. Aunt Christine still talks about it fondly even though she moved out long ago. Her bedroom is on the first floor, directly across from the dining room. If you ever visit the home, you can see her original furniture is there today.

❦

Of course, "home" has little to do with physical buildings and virtually everything to do with the spirit of the people who live in that space. So many people make the terrible mistake of believing they need to have a huge mansion or the latest and fanciest of everything before they can be happy. They think that material goods define them, and therefore lose the chance to make strong and lasting connections with their loved ones because they're busily in pursuit of those material goods. My daddy used to say people spend more time trying to make a living than they do making a life, and that's especially true when you think about how people try to fill their houses with symbols of wealth.

A home doesn't have to be a mansion. The smallest, humblest place can have the same charm and beauty a mansion might have. A home is beautiful if it reflects and inspires the personalities of the people who live in it—if there are delicious smells emanating from the kitchen; if there's the sound of laughter and play in the air; if it's clear from the sense of order and the good condition of all—that creates the loving environment. If this is the case, then we can know the people in the home love and respect each other because home is the place where agape love should abide.

A home is a palace when every person knows that he or she belongs and is loved. Of course, our parents' bedrooms and office spaces can have certain boundaries, and we can learn to respect a closed door and knock before entering someone's private space. Yet one should never feel "shut out" at home. Then, too, we must respect the fact that while many people enjoy community, there is also a time for sanctuary. The home should be a sanctuary whether we live alone or within a family unit. And there should be times for togetherness and time alone.

In our family, because so many of us have been called to be warriors, we look for love and peace at home. Those qualities are a premium, along with honor, respect, forgiveness, and so many things discussed in this chapter.

Agreement should exist between the heads of the family. In our family we side with Joshua 24:15:

> If it is disagreeable in your sight to serve the LORD,
> choose for yourselves today whom you will serve:
> whether the gods which your fathers served which
> were beyond the River, or the gods of the Amorites
> in whose land you are living; but as for me and my
> house, we will serve the LORD. (NASB)

I think we are most capable of creating a home when we take heed of Joshua's words. I also think Daddy King's words add something. Granddaddy once said:

> Yes, money is important, and it's a whole lot easier
> to get by when you have it than when you don't, but
> if money inhibits you from living your life—from
> creating a real home for yourself and your family—
> then that's a terrible trade-off.

Words and messages like this are among the most important types of lessons that I learned at home while growing up. At home I learned that life is sacred. I learned that all people are created equal in God's eyes. I learned that there is only one human race, with each member in need of a loving and merciful God and His Son Jesus. These truths were reinforced when I attended church, and school too (prayer wasn't banned until 1963). But our home—where the Holy Bible and the Author of the book were honored—was always the bastion for truth.

For us, in the King family, a real home has God at the heart of it. God is love, and love abounds in a home where God is honored. In our family rooms, around our kitchen and dining room tables, at our bedside on our knees, we talk about God and we talk to God. We pray together in corporate settings, and we pray alone with God in our secret places in our homes.

Home is about knowing that there are such certain truths as these; knowing that spiritual values—God-honoring values—are so much more important than any material possessions will ever be; knowing that if God isn't at the center of our beings, we aren't really going to become or achieve anything truly worthwhile. The spiritual value of all existence should be very evident in every home.

HOME: A PLACE WHERE GOODNESS GROWS

Home is a place where families dwell together;
Or where the one alone can learn to live with God.
Home can be a social place, where friends are welcome.
The door swings open two ways,
Bringing love in and taking love out;
To a desperate world in need.
God should live at home with you, then blessings too
*   can flow.*
Beauty, courage, honor, joy should rest inside your door.
There is a garden we call home, where good character
*   can surely grow.*
With purpose, faith, humility, wisdom, and honor in
*   our soil,*
We learn to thank the God of grace for Heaven's
*   abundant oil.*
Home is a place where goodness grows, when Jesus is
*   invited in.*
Let's pray for Love and Peace and Grace, and
*   family homes. Amen.*

RULE NO. 2

Serve Your Family

My uncle and my father were great, powerful, and inspiring men. They were at the
forefront of one of the most important
movements in the history of America or, for that matter, the history of humankind. That much is, of course,
part of the public record. What isn't known nearly as
well is the great, powerful, and inspiring roles they
served within our homes, and how those roles are links
in a chain that unites several generations of our family.

In our family the men have always stood at the head,
true patriarchs that take the lead, teach, and live their
lives as examples. We were taught, practically from the
time we left the womb, that our fathers knew best for
all of us.

Of course, this doesn't mean that women are not clearly and dearly respected in our family. Women have a significant role as helpers to our husbands and co-counsels in the parental equation. It is just that the women in our family, our mothers and grandmothers, were always wise and able to know the value of their strategic roles as wives and mothers. The roles of matriarch and patriarch are distinct, and in the King family we have been blessed with strong examples of both.

In the late twentieth and early twenty-first centuries, the family template has changed quite a bit. There are single-parent homes where children grow up without having the experience of living under the loving influence of both parents. This situation bears much prayer and necessitates much encouragement for those parents who have the unique burden of raising children in this manner. Because of that I want to spend some time here painting a picture of what the roles of patriarch and matriarch can mean to a family.

❧

How does a man become a real patriarch? The most effective way is by following the lead of the men who came before him, especially when he comes from a line of truly great men. I can illustrate that through the line that led to my father and my uncle.

We can begin with Willis Williams, a preaching slave. He knew something about the Bible, so his slave master, William N. Williams, allowed him to preach to other slaves. On January 2, 1863, the day after President Lincoln signed the Emancipation Proclamation, Willis, his wife, Lucretia, their young son, Adam, and his twin sister, Eve, became a free family. My great-grandfather, Dr. Adam Daniel Williams, was born as a slave around 1861, but as a free man he chose to record January 2, 1863, as his birthday.

Great-granddaddy wanted to preach like his daddy, so he started his ministry at seven years old. He would practice his sermons using the community children as his congregation members, and he preached at the funerals of pets—snakes, cats, dogs, horses, or anything else that died. The neighborhood called on him whenever the opportunity arose, and they responded with shouts and applause. Though he was unable to attend school because of the demands of sharecropping, Great-granddaddy reportedly attracted the people for miles around with his ability to count and cipher.

Along with his dream of preaching, Great-granddaddy also desired a better life for himself and the family he dreamed of having. He earned his license to preach in April 1888, and he tried to make a living as an itinerant preacher during the late 1880s and early 1890s while supplementing his income with other work. But then a sawmill accident left him with only the nub of a thumb on his right hand. Believing there was a better life out there somewhere, he joined the black exodus from Greene County, Georgia, and headed for Atlanta in January 1893, where he met and married a school-teacher, Jenny Celeste Parks.

Great-granddaddy received his doctorate from Morehouse College and became a pillar of the community. He cofounded and became president of the Atlanta chapter of the NAACP, became the pastor of Ebenezer Baptist Church, and helped to establish Washington High School, a place where black children could pursue excellence in education.

He also became mentor to Michael Luther "Big Mike" King, the grandson of an Irish sharecropper and a freed African slave woman. It was with Great-granddaddy that Big Mike discovered his calling to preach—along with Dr. Williams's daughter. When Great-granddaddy died, Mike became the pastor of Ebenezer Baptist Church.

Daddy King and Big Mama soon had their first boy

and named him Michael Luther King Jr. That name stuck for a short while, but one day Big Mike made a powerful decision. According to family lore, his mother had wanted to name him Martin Luther after the famous Reformation preacher. However, her Caucasian midwife thought that the name was "too fine for a Negro boy" and wrote "Michael Luther" on the birth certificate instead. Now that he was a father himself, Mike went down to the courthouse and changed his name and his son's name to Martin Luther King.

I want to pause here and underline that for you. Great-granddaddy chose his birthday as the day he became a free man, and Granddaddy gave himself a new name. Those are both admirable pictures of self-possession and pride. No wonder Uncle M.L. and my father, A.D., were such strong men. They had generations of powerful role models as they themselves became patriarchs in their homes and in their communities. And in our households, they, like the men who came before them, were the unquestioned leaders.

Now, as I said before, this is not to suggest in any way that the women in the family were weak or subservient.

And certainly subservience is not a role I have any interest in playing.

Anyone who got to see my Aunt Coretta in action and could imagine her as subservient has a much wilder imagination than I do. The same has always been true for Big Mama King, Aunt Christine, and even my mother. These women all had their interests and careers outside the home, yet the role of homemaker was never abandoned in their lives. For example, Mother, Aunt Christine, and Aunt Coretta were all concert singers in the days of the civil rights movement. During her lifetime, Aunt Coretta founded the King Center. Aunt Christine founded the Alberta King Scholarship Fund. My mother, Naomi, founded the A.D. King Foundation in honor of my father's work with youth and nonviolent social change.

While men have always stood at the heads of our family units, women have consistently had intensely vital roles. They have been close confidantes of their husbands. They have been prayer partners of their husbands. And they have had strong and strongly individual voices.

The operating structure that has thrived in my family for generations is one I consider to be an ideal model because I know how well it has worked. It revolves around a mother and father both living in the home and both taking active, hands-on roles in all key family decisions.

For generations this collaboration extended to day-to-day child rearing. For example, Daddy King and Mama King were very much equal partners in this regard. This changed in my father and uncle's generation because their work in the civil rights movement was so extensive that they were often away from the home for long stretches. Still, they maintained very strong levels of authority and took very active roles in their children's lives.

This was certainly true with my father and me. My daddy liked to bring us on adventures and take us to movies like *Superman* and *Hercules* that fed our sense of adventure. He was a champion swimmer, and he loved to take us to the beach.

One of my most memorable stories from childhood was when my family went to a spiritual event in Pensacola, Florida. During some time away from the event, my daddy took us to the ocean. The waves were big, but I had no fear of them. Part of this was because I thought they were so beautiful and majestic. Another part was because my father was right there with me. Knowing what a great swimmer he was, I knew I had nothing to fear in the water.

It wasn't my intention to test this, but I found the waves alluring. I knew how to swim a little bit, and the temptation to frolic proved too great. My frolic turned to fright, however, when I realized the waves had taken me out into the ocean and I wasn't strong enough to get back to shore. Before I could start to panic, though, I spotted my daddy cutting through the waves like they were mere ripples. Within moments he had his arm around me and was guiding me back to safety. I can remember Daddy's sermons about Jesus walking on the water. When Daddy preached about Jesus, his Holy Spirit–inspired lessons made a believer out of me. When Daddy swam out to get me, I likely expected to see Jesus walking along beside him.

That story symbolizes so much for me. Obviously, it represents the vision I always had of my father as an immensely strong figure looking over me, but it also represents the place the men have always had at the head of our families. They're the guardians, the ones who step in when life threatens to become too dangerous. They lead with strength and with resolve. The men (and women) in our family have strong faith in God. Neither the devastation of violence nor the degradation of time has diminished the effect my father, my uncle, and my grandfather had on our family

structure—the example passed down through generations is that strong.

***

In our family, a father's most important role is to make
his children feel safe and secure. In the tumult of the
times I grew up in, that required extraordinary effort,
but my father nevertheless pulled it off. I always had the
sense, even when the movement took him far from home,
that my father was watching over me. I can't say that I
was always delighted about this—teenagers want their
freedom, after all—but I can say it was always a comfort,
at least in the back of my mind.

One day when we had a family dinner at Uncle M.L.'s
house, I decided to slip around and follow him as he
moved about the house. I was a curious girl and wanted to
know more about this uncle who was always in the news.
I tried to be invisible, but he was on to my game from the
start. When he excused himself from the family to step
into his study for a moment, I slipped behind him and
peeked around the doorway of his office. He sat down,
stretched his arms above his head, and breathed a sigh of
relief to have that quiet moment alone. I came in and held
out his house shoes to him. As he kicked off his shoes and

stepped into his slippers, he chuckled in that deep and gentle voice of his. His smile was as bright as sunshine. "Ah, Alveda," he said. "You are such a pretty girl. And you're growing up. We're going to have to chase the boys away one day."

That assurance, knowing that he was looking out for me, just as Daddy and Granddaddy were, was so comforting. It was always like that in their presence. They made me feel so safe and so loved. That's the way it was in our family growing up. The women looking after the children and the men. The men watching over and protecting us. God watching over and caring for us all.

On occasion I would rebel and my father would decide to allow me to range around a little. Whether or not he intended it this way, this would always lead to some sort of lesson for me. For example, when it was time for my senior prom, my father announced that he was going to drive my date and me to the event and then be there to pick us up afterward. As a high schooler about to go off to college, this idea was completely unpalatable to me.

"Daddy, you can't do that," I said emphatically. "Nobody does that; that's so old-fashioned."

My father didn't take kindly to my rejecting his

protection. I don't think he was particularly happy about my calling him old-fashioned either, as he was still a young man. Still, I continued to insist, and he eventually let my date drive some of my friends and me. As things happened, we were out very late, my date fell asleep behind the wheel, and we got into an accident. Fortunately, no one was hurt, but Daddy didn't miss the opportunity to use this as a "teaching moment," making it clear that no such calamity would have befallen us if we'd let him drive us.

The other important thing all the King men did for their children was make them feel cherished and loved. Daddy found every opportunity he could to show me that he believed I was special. When I became a teenager, he bought me pearl earrings as a way to mark my transition to womanhood.

When I turned sixteen, he threw me a big Sweet Sixteen party and made me feel like I was the belle of the ball. I used to wonder why the boys in our crowd never tried to sneak me into the corners for a kiss. Later I learned that my daddy had a way of scaring them off. It became a big joke: "Girl, you are the prettiest girl around, but your daddy has a way of praying that makes us think twice," they would say.

"Of course I'm nonviolent," he laughed and said.

"But don't forget what happened to the boys who picked on the prophet."

Uncle M.L. wasn't my father, but our families were very close, which meant I spent a great deal of time with my uncle and aunt and could see how his parenting style mirrored my father's. I would babysit for him and Aunt Coretta on Sundays after we all went to church, so I also had the opportunity to witness many of his stirring sermons up close. The thing I think of first when I think of my uncle is the extraordinary power of his oratory, delivered in one of the most beautiful voices God has ever granted a human being.

Aunt Christine taught me how to sew, and how to manage a career and homemaking at the same time. She had so many neat recipes that could be cooked in a flash and still taste good. Her Sock-It-To-Me cake was stirred up out of a box, but she added cabinet spices and made it seem homemade.

Mama taught me how to make biscuits when I was twelve. She let me help in the kitchen when she and my God-Mama were preparing for a catering event. Mama had a home business of catering and interior design because Daddy didn't want her working full-time. They had a special arrangement, those two. Daddy would do all of the dangerous frontline civil rights work, and

Mama would maintain a safe and loving home environment. This is such a special tribute of the love that two parents can have for each other and their children.

❧

One of the things I feel is so important in making a family run properly is being sure that everyone is aware of what is expected of him or her and what kind of contribution he or she needs to make. Going back several generations, the King family children have known where they stood and how things worked. They were taught the value of sharing prayer in the home from the time they were very little, and as they got older, each of them went to vacation Bible school during the summer.

In the home we were taught to honor and obey parental authority, and to also obey proper authority outside the home. This included the school, church, and social environments. Yes, we were taught to honor our fathers and mothers. This didn't mean we couldn't express questions about or try to negotiate our way around the rules or regulations—and I certainly did more than my share of that on occasion—but it did mean we had to accept that our parents were the heads of the house and their decisions were final. We were actually encouraged to ask respectful questions, but once our parents made the final decisions, the buck stopped there.

We called all of our elders *sir* and *ma'am* as a sign of respect. We were also taught that this was not something we should do simply out of obligation. We did it out of acknowledgment of their wisdom and appreciation for what they could teach us.

Discipline was meted out firmly, and disobedience was punished. On occasion my mother felt the need to spank us, and my father even brought out the belt a few times, but these were never done maliciously and, in retrospect, I could see how their actions were justified; sometimes we just got a little too raucous for our own good.

My uncle believed it was essential that we nurture the children—but not at the expense of teaching them to be good and responsible citizens. "It is quite true," he once wrote,

> that many modern parents go too far in allowing their children to express themselves with hardly a modicum of discipline. . . . This almost "lunatic fringe" of modern childcare has been responsible

for most strange and fantastic methods of child rearing in many American homes. The child must realize that there are rules of the game which he did not make and that he cannot break with impunity.

(ADVICE FOR LIVING, MARCH 1958)

In my adulthood I've come to appreciate the wisdom of this approach to discipline. In my opinion it is essential that you teach children right when they are young, because if you haven't worked with them and established a sense of right, wrong, and authority by the time they're about seven years old, you're going to be in trouble.

Because of this, I'll be very firm with my little grandchildren, whom I love dearly. When my three-year-old granddaughter—a child with a very strong will—acts up, I sit her in a chair and say, "I want you to sit there and I want you to think about making the right choice and making the wrong choice. If you make the right choice, you're gonna be happy. If you make the wrong choice, you're either gonna wind up spanked or sitting in a chair by yourself." To my delight, she's making better choices all the time.

The King family attitude about the relationship between husbands and wives might seem a bit retro, but it has endured and evolved with the times, and in many ways has always been well ahead of its time. Since I was the Sunday babysitter, I got to see Uncle M.L. and Aunt Coretta's relationship up close regularly. Here's a scene I saw play out on numerous occasions: M.L. would come back from the church, having given his all on the pulpit. By the time he arrived, Aunt Coretta would have his slippers sitting next to his chair in his study. M.L. would kiss his wife and children and then repair to his study to find a little bit of quiet and meditation for himself. Meanwhile, my aunt would go into the kitchen to prepare dinner and give him some time for peaceful reflection.

Was this scene something out of *Ozzie and Harriet*? I suppose it was to some degree, but that was only one important part of the picture. At the domestic level, the King women have always tried to make their husbands feel pampered, and that let the men know their wives were attentive to their needs.

As I mentioned, though, we've always had a progressive sensibility when it comes to gender roles, and this played out outside of the home. Aunt Coretta embraced her role as a housewife, but that was only one of her roles.

She was the model of the modern career woman and the model of the traditional housewife at the same time, and she saw no contradiction in this. This has continued to be true in my generation and in my children's generation as well. King women are all very well developed and secure in who they are, but they also value the role of the husband as the patriarch. They were not made to feel less as women, but they appreciated their roles as helpmeets. To me, that is extraordinarily healthy for a family.

In terms of all major family decisions, those have been collaborations between husband and wife in our households for as long as I can tell. Certainly this was the model Daddy King and Mama King provided. Even as a child, I could see them working together whenever an important choice had to be made. This changed a bit in my parents' generation because my father and uncle were gone so much, but even then the parents discussed options regarding the home, the children, and finances whenever feasible.

RULE NO. 3

Get a Good Education

B eyond instilling in every child a strong foundation of faith (which works by agape love because God is love), I can't think of a more important strategy than providing our young with the kind of education that leads to giving them a real chance to do something meaningful with their lives.

As is true with so many of my beliefs, this value comes from my forebears. And like the other values we hold so dear, the King family has always "walked the talk" when it comes to education. Mama King's mother was a schoolteacher. Her aunt was a schoolteacher as well. Mama King herself was a teacher, and after she retired she set up a scholarship fund to continue to bless students.

Aunt Christine, Daddy and Uncle M.L.'s "big sister," followed her mama's and grandmama's examples and became a teacher. Aunt Christine was a leader among teachers in those days. And she still teaches at the prestigious Spelman College, although she is well into her active eighties. Aunt Christine and my mother are so amazing and vibrant in their golden years. Mother wasn't a teacher, but because she had been an honor roll student, she always served as a great model for us as students.

As a young elementary school teacher, Aunt Christine was excited about applying many of the innovative education strategies that were slow to be embraced in Southern segregated school systems. I was one of her early subjects, and she taught me to read before I was five. Today such a testimony isn't so remarkable as children often read at very young ages now, but back then we were mavericks. Years later, when my first son was born, thanks to Aunt Christine's guidance he was reading the front page of the newspaper with comprehension by the time he was five.

I later became a teacher, and my two daughters did as well. My son was also a teacher before starting his legal career. My youngest daughter is a creative teacher, whose teaching style reminds me of Aunt Christine's.

She, like our aunt has always done, takes young proté-gées under her wing and guides them along the path to success.

It would take another book to tell you about my nineteen years as a college professor. Suffice it to say that though I left that post several years ago, I still feel a sense of blessing whenever I meet former students who today are among the ranks of mayors, financial advisors, corporate managers, and ministers of the gospel of Jesus Christ.

⌘

Education is not only important to our family; it is a critical part of the fabric of our family. The Kings have always been and will always be steeped in the belief that a vital society is built on the bedrock of good education.

My uncle spoke often and eloquently about this. To me, he captured the essence of our perspective on the topic when he wrote, "The function of education is to teach one to think intensively and to think critically. Intelligence plus character—that is the goal of true education." What he was identifying here were the two most important functions of education: developing keen minds and developing strong moral standards. I know quite a few teachers, and I strongly believe that most of them feel these are the twin functions of any good school system. However, I'm not nearly as convinced that school administrations and our government feel the same way.

Since the public school system began, it has been the foundation of education in America. It is essential that this be the case because far too many people in this country could never afford even a minimal education without public schools—and education should never be considered a luxury that only the rich can pay for. However, public schools have gone so far in stripping any expression of faith from their premises that they can no longer provide the moral example that is so necessary to give our children.

While it is not something that I believe, I can appreciate and defend the right of parents to choose for their children schools that are completely devoid of religious teaching. However, as this is the only choice in our public schools, I think the vast majority of our students are being improperly served. Furthermore, this goes against the wishes of their families. I strongly believe parents should be able to select a form of education for their children that mirrors their own values, including prayer in schools if parents so desire. I was discussing this with my daughter, Darlene Celeste, the other day, and she came up with an idea that I think is absolutely brilliant.

"There should be magnet schools for each faith and ones for no faith at all," she said to me, continuing:

> The schools should fit the designs of the family, not the family fitting the designs of the schools or the government. We should have a voucher system that lets parents send their kids where they believe they should go. There should be magnet Christian schools and Jewish schools and Buddhist schools. And there should be schools for those who only want to believe in science or just those who want to keep belief out of it entirely.

While I think she's right to search for a solution, I believe that my elders would say that if we would take the loving role of evangelism more to heart, we wouldn't need too many of those types of schools.

So while I don't agree with forbidding the allowance of prayer in schools, I also know we can't legislate salvation. It would be wiser to encourage solutions that would allow children to pray voluntarily in schools, especially at mealtimes, and teachers as well. When

Mama King and Daddy King went to school, their schools were church-based, from elementary level all the way through college. Their children went to both public schools and private schools, but back then, before 1963, prayer wasn't outlawed in public schools. I think if it had been, my grandparents would have moved M.L., A.D., and Christine immediately because the public schools no longer matched our natural family values.

I sent three of my children to Christian schools, and my oldest son graduated from Oral Roberts, a Christian college. Two of my other children got their law degrees from Liberty University. We have always believed that education should follow the structure and philosophies of the family, where in our case natural life, marriage, and family values follow the biblical worldview. However, we had the means to provide natural moral values incorporated into formal education through private schools. So much of the population can't do that, and they shouldn't suffer because of it.

❧

Some people go so far as to advocate closing all public schools in favor of private schools and home schooling. While it is understandable that frustration with failing schools drives this line of thinking, there must be a better way.

Let's face it: today many parents expect the schools to raise their children. And what children don't learn from school, they learn from their peers and entertainment on TV, on the radio, at the movies, and on the Internet. Heaven forbid! It is not the job of the school to raise our children. Schools do not raise children; parents do. While the teachers and administrators of schools can make academic corrections in the lives of our children, they should not be required to discipline our children. If the children are not raised and disciplined properly at home, then any education plan is bound for failure. When I was growing up, we were never confused regarding the role of the schools and the role of "home training."

This training needs to extend to showing children how to be responsible members of a school community. When teachers spend the majority of their time simply trying to keep their students in line, everyone suffers. It is our job as parents to insist our children be obedient to proper authority in the classrooms, to obey their teachers no matter what other students are doing. Meanwhile, parents need to be aware of peer pressure and how certain companionship can corrupt good manners and the family's hard work of training the children.

In our family we teach our children to be leaders, to be godly examples among their peers. When I was growing up I would ask to do something because all my friends were doing it. I remember begging for a popular style of penny loafers because all the kids seemed to be wearing them. Never mind that the style was bad for my wide, flat feet; I just had to have them. My mother responded with something like this: "The fact that everyone seems to be doing a thing doesn't make it right. If they all jump off a bridge, are you planning to jump too?" Still, she got the shoes for me. They looked terrible on my feet, but Mama made me wear them anyway, saying, "Don't you know that money doesn't grow on trees?" I was enough of a smart aleck to say that paper is made out of wood, and wood is part of trees, but Mama's discipline was strong and she always had the last word in a matter.

When our lessons resonate in our children's lives, this means they will not follow the world's example but will rather lead by God's example. If we train them well in the paths they should follow in their early days, when they grow up they will not depart from that training; and if they do for a little while, we pray they will remember and return to their training. When children learn early in life that they can be leaders—not followers of the examples of their peers or other humans, but rather following the Word of God—they can be set free from harmful peer pressure.

All of this comes back to creating an environment in which schools can foster our children. That said, we need a new approach to the choices available in public schools and a new commitment to the union of values and education. This isn't just an ideal; it has gotten to the point where it is imperative.

It is impossible to think of a bright future for our children without the benefit of a good education. Yet so many of our schools are little more than holding tanks for our children before we pour them out onto the streets.

There is no excuse for our failure to educate every one of our children; each of them has the potential to contribute so much to the world. We have the resources at our disposal. It is our obligation to deploy them in such a way that our young people can learn to think intensively and critically and make the positive mark they are meant to make on our society. The ideological wars that use our children as political footballs are unjust. We must find honest measures that will allow families the comfort and security of knowing that all school systems, public, private, parochial, and home-based, are founded and grounded on the same principles—those of providing excellent education for all children.

～ッ～

We are losing far too many of our young people to jail. I strongly believe there are two reasons for this. One is the lack of the kind of strong family structure I talked about in the last chapter. The other is the failure of many schools to serve as a place where great character is both modeled and emphasized. While this is important for a child who comes from a home with good values, it is doubly important when those values are lacking in the home. As a society we can't condemn our children to repeating the mistakes of their parents when we can help them avoid those mistakes.

Now, I've already said schools can't be the only place where children learn discipline, principles, and morals. And I have certainly seen far too many parents drop their kids off at school and effectively say, "You raise them." But the reality is children often spend more of their waking hours with their teachers than they do with their parents, and those teachers need to send a strong and unwavering message about character. Certainly, it is my preference that this message be sent through the gospel of Jesus Christ, but I understand that not everyone shares my specific faith. What is most important—non-negotiable, in my opinion—is that some form of values education be in place in all of our public schools, even those that choose to keep religion completely out of their curriculum.

My uncle understood this. In "The Purpose of Education," written in the late forties, he said, "The most dangerous criminal may be the man gifted with reason, but with no morals." His point is the same point I'm making now: that it isn't enough to teach a person what is correct; it is also vitally important we teach people what is right. "We must remember that intelligence is not enough," M.L. continued, adding:

> Intelligence plus character—that is the goal of true education. The complete education gives one not only power of concentration, but worthy objectives upon which to concentrate. The broad education will, therefore, transmit to one not only the accumulated knowledge of the race but also the accumulated experience of social living.

My uncle also felt strongly that we don't do enough to prioritize a good education for all in America. In 1964 he received the John Dewey Award from the United Federation of Teachers. In his acceptance speech he said the following:

> The richest nation on Earth has never allocated enough resources to build sufficient schools, to compensate adequately its teachers, and to surround them with the prestige our work justifies. We squander funds on highways, on the frenetic pursuit of recreation, on the overabundance of overkill armament, but we pauperize education. (NOTES FOR UNITED FEDERATION OF TEACHERS ADDRESS)

This is yet another place where M.L. was speaking for all the Kings who came before him with words that we continue to uphold to this day. It pains me to see so many school systems under severe budget crises using out-of-date textbooks and failing equipment. Taking arts and enhancement programs from our children robs them of the opportunity to experience the many learning pleasures that extend beyond the three R's. And when classrooms are filled to bursting with students because a school system can't afford to hire enough teachers, then we lose both the students and the teachers—because no one can learn effectively in such a situation, and the joy of teaching is lost when there are so many minds to address at once.

～

I don't believe we can truly make the most of ourselves as a people until we accept that providing our children with a great education is one of our highest priorities. Much is made in other circles about the trickle-down effect of various policies, but there can be little question about the trickle-down effect of providing each child with a quality education. Well-educated children grow up to be significant contributors to society. Well-educated children are much less likely to commit crimes and expect handouts. Well-educated children raise the conscience of the entire country. What trickles down from great education is undeniable: a world we would all prefer to live in.

High-quality public education should never be on the losing end of the numbers game when it comes to doling out financial resources. Other than ensuring the safety and security of our citizens, there is no public service more important. Therefore, when it's time to slash budgets on the national or local level, we need to decide that the education budget is one of the very last to be touched. We need to stop—as my uncle put so eloquently—"pauperizing education."

At the same time we need to find a way to offer our teachers the best possible training and a way to make a wage commensurate with their contribution to society. The average teacher's salary in America is similar to what the average bartender makes. Now, I'm sure most bartenders have helped their share of people over time, but my guess is that most teachers have helped quite a few more. That teachers and bartenders earn even close to the same amount of money when teachers are responsible for the very minds of our children is a clear indication of how grossly we undervalue our educators.

I've heard it argued that teachers don't deserve higher salaries because they only work ten months out of the year. My guess is that anyone who makes this argument hasn't spent any time teaching. For one thing, teachers work incredibly hard during those ten months, often planning lessons or grading papers late into the night. For another, very few of them spend those other two months sipping cocktails poolside. In many cases, they're working another job during the summer because their teaching salaries are so low.

The other critical reason why we need to raise teacher salaries is that doing so will increase the chance that the best and brightest will want to become teachers. Many people go into teaching now because it is their calling, and I applaud all of them, but too many other talented college graduates stay away from teaching even though they might be great at it and might love it because they know they can't make a decent living at it. In most metropolitan areas teachers can't afford to own a home on their salaries. Why would the best candidates choose this option? More to the point, why would we make them choose this option?

This is what my uncle was referring to when he talked about pauperizing education. We provide our schools with the trappings of paupers, we pay our teachers barely better than paupers, and we somehow expect them to turn out a generation of princes. It just doesn't make sense, and we need to do better.

CHILDREN LEARN WHAT THEY LIVE

If children live with criticism, they learn to
   condemn.
If children live with hostility, they learn to fight.
If children live with ridicule, they learn to be shy.
If children live with shame, they learn to feel guilty.
If children live with encouragement, they learn
   confidence.
If children live with tolerance, they learn to be patient.
If children live with praise, they learn to appreciate.
If children live with acceptance, they learn to love.
If children live with approval, they learn to love.
If children live with honesty, they learn truthfulness.
If children live with security, they learn to have faith in
   themselves and others.
If children live with friendliness, they learn the
   world is a nice place in which to live.

Dorothy Law Nolte, PhD

RULE NO. 4

Guard Your Heart

Most people know my uncle as a stirring orator capable of bringing unequaled wisdom to some of the biggest global issues of his time. He was a world-changer, someone capable of looking at enormously complex issues and showing the way to right crippling wrongs. However, he was also a husband, a father, and a family man, and he had some wise thoughts about interpersonal matters. Though perhaps not as visionary as his greatest speeches, these thoughts still ring true decades after he expressed them.

Such is the case with Uncle M.L.'s thoughts about romance. He'd spoken often among the family and on the pulpit about why marriage is so important, and how people should wait for sex until marriage. Though he didn't speak much about it in his public speeches, *Ebony* magazine asked him to do an advice column called "Advice for Living" from 1957 to 1958, and there he had the opportunity to go on the record about issues I know meant a great deal to him.

Perhaps his most telling bit of advice came in response to a question from a woman who, at age twenty-nine, was still a virgin but had begun to question the value of staying a virgin until she found a husband. There are many men and women today, even much younger, who need to take Uncle M.L.'s words to heart.

"I think you should hold firm to the principle of premarital virginity," he wrote in his November 1957 column, adding:

> The problems created by premarital sex relationships are far greater than the problems created by premarital virginity. The suspicion, fears, and guilt feelings generated by premarital sex relations are contributing factors to the present breakdown of the family. Real men still respect purity and virginity within women. If a man breaks a relationship with you because you would not allow him to participate in the sexual act, you can be assured that he did not love you from the beginning.

My uncle answered this young woman perfectly, and I have taken his advice a step further with my sons and grandsons. The simple fact is, if a man wants to marry a virgin but spends his unmarried life sleeping around, there won't be many virgins left to marry. Young men as well as young women need to make it their mission to guard their purity.

I have had the good fortune to witness several wonderful, loving relationships in my family. I saw one in my very own home between my mother and father. Though they'd only been married nineteen years when my father died under suspicious circumstances shortly after my uncle's assassination (he was found dead in our home swimming pool with no water in his lungs and a bruise on his head, clearly a victim of murder), the time they had together was one of great sharing and love.

As a child I watched my father come home and seek refuge from his difficult days in my mother's arms. The two of them would kneel and pray together, finding enormous strength in their shared connection with God. Many years after he died, my mother told me that praying together reminded them on a daily basis just how special and blessed their relationship was.

The Lord has granted my Aunt Christine and Uncle Isaac many, many more years together. They recently celebrated their fiftieth wedding anniversary in grand fashion with the entire family around them. My aunt and uncle have been through more than their share of trials over the years, but they have had an enduring, sustaining love that still brings a blush to their cheeks when they look at each other. It's impossible not to find inspiration in this. Like my mother and father, my aunt and uncle have always prayed together, and they point to this as a key to the longevity of their union.

I don't think this is coincidental. Research has shown that people who are in monogamous Christian marriages live longer. The common bond of faith gives couples a connection that holds them together, that inspires them, and that gives them something to reach toward in unison. When a man and woman pray and worship together, they are touching each other on a higher level. By extending their hearts to God, they're opening themselves to otherwise unattainable levels of joy. At the same time they are offering their marriage and their family up to God's protection. This makes the difficult times so much easier to navigate and keeps husband and wife pointed in the same direction at all times.

Romance always abounded in our family. Daddy King called his bride Alberta "Honey Bunch." When they were courting, Granddaddy was always trying to steal a kiss. One evening when the family was headed to church, Big Mama was suffering from a slight headache and decided to stay home. Granddaddy was at church hoping to see her. When he didn't, he realized this was one of the rare occasions Big Mama was at home alone without her protective parents. It was his chance. He slipped away from the service, ran down the block and a half to the house, slipped around to the side, and knocked on her window. She was surprised to see him, but he put on his best Romeo and talked her into giving him a little kiss. He was back to church in time for the benediction, happier than anything. It was the start of an affection that lasted the rest of their lives.

Uncle M.L. often sent Coretta flowers from the road along with letters of endearment. Nathan King, Daddy King's Irish grandfather, defied the racism of his day and married a freed slave woman named Malinde. Since Caucasians couldn't marry Negroes back then, their marriage ceremony involved a slave tradition called "jumping the broom." Their blessed love resulted in the marriage of their son James Albert King to Delia Lindsay, the parents of Daddy King.

I wish everyone had the opportunity to experience the same thing.

~∙~

Big Mama King gave me my first book about sex and marriage, entitled *For Girls Only*. That book contained so much information from a godly perspective that I was convinced that I should wait for sex until after marriage. As a result Daddy walked a virgin down the aisle.

Sadly, what I've seen with my parents and so many others in my family is far too often the exception. Today young people are led to believe that sex and marriage are not sacred or even related. The procreative purpose of sexual attraction is secondary, and often nonexistent. The anything goes, consequence-free mentality that prevails leads to emotionally deficient sexual encounters that often take the participants down a path to multiple sexual partners, divorce, disease, abortion, and dwindling chances for true intimacy.

The way I understand the Bible, marriage is for procreation, sexual fellowship and enjoyment, and bodily ministry between one man and one woman. But as

Christians we have not effectively taught our young people about God's plan and the rewards that come from fulfilling it. Our sons and daughters value their cell phones, iPods, gold chains, cars, and clothes much more than they value their own bodies, which are the temples of the Holy Ghost. It is critical that we reverse this thinking as quickly as possible.

The situation is not hopeless, though. I have seen some very positive signs. As a mother, minister, and family relationships counselor, I have experienced an increasingly favorable response to my encouragements for abstinence, chastity, sexual purity, and marriage. The faithful ranks of believers who cling to Christ's teaching about the sanctity of marriage and the true role of godly sex are being fortified by a new generation committed to purity.

When talking to teenagers about this subject, I find it most effective to liken premarital virginity to waiting until Christmas morning to open your presents. It may sound simplistic, but when I ask kids what they remember about the time leading up to the moment when they got their gifts, they recall the joy of anticipation, and they tell me they appreciated their gifts so much more because the excitement generated by waiting heightened the experience for them. When I explain that waiting for sex until marriage can generate the same sense of fulfillment, I see heads nodding all over the room. With this simple analogy, they begin to understand the true value in delayed gratification, especially when dealing with something as precious as this.

Of course, that doesn't mean if you wait for your spouse, your first time together will be magical. But you have a lifetime to practice, and what could be better than that?

The most romantic love stories in the Bible are between married people. When I seek divine inspiration on this topic, I need to look no further than the Song of Solomon, and the line, "Promise me, O women of Jerusalem, not to awaken love until the time is right" (8:4 NLT). To me, this line clearly says that love and sex can only be fulfilling and right when it comes as a result of patience, temperance, and purity of heart.

If we awaken our instincts to love before marriage—allowing our passions to control us—we will experience the consequences of love at the wrong time and perhaps never understand the unmatched joy that comes with true love.

The biggest challenge we face as a society is the lie perpetuated by the mass media and organizations like Planned Parenthood that it is impossible or unrealistic to wait until marriage to have sex. It is no more impossible to remain chaste until marriage than it is to remain true to your country or to put the concerns of others ahead of your own. People do it all the time, and they experience joys from this that others will never know.

Those who promote having multiple sexual partners diminish the value of sex. I suppose that's where the phrase "free love" originates. The counterfeit sex without commitment is so cheap as to have no worth at all. What some fail to understand is that the ability to look into your spouse's eyes and know that no one has ever looked at this person the same way is a blessing everyone should get to experience. There are few things in the world that are truly irreplaceable. This is one of them.

I know this to be the case firsthand, sadly, because I strayed from the family values as a young woman. After divorcing at an early age, I entered into other relationships, and the almost mystical bond of my first—and what should have been my only—sexual relationship in life was broken. I never recaptured it.

Now I have to use my life as an example of what not to do, and to urge others to learn from my mistakes. My mistakes spilled over into the lives of my children as well, and thank God that I have learned to pray over my children and their marriages, and to do my very best to keep my unmarried children on the path to sexual purity. They have their trials, though. We all depend on the mercy of God.

Just as Song of Solomon teaches us about the virtues of premarital purity, Proverbs 5:18 speaks volumes about fidelity: "May your fountain be blessed, and may you rejoice in the wife of your youth" (NIV). The message of this passage is we should stay true to those to whom we have vowed to be faithful. Infidelity is a dreadfully ruinous act with devastating consequences. Sex outside of marriage not only denies the sacred function of sex, but it also repudiates the vows taken before God to give your heart and soul exclusively to your betrothed.

I've known very few marriages that have withstood the degradations of infidelity. I believe this is true because, for most people with an actively functioning conscience, it is impossible to separate the *act* of sex from the *intimacy* of sex. Once that intimacy is debased by the introduction of a third party (or more), it suffers a wound that is almost always fatal.

Back in my father's day, he and my uncle were traveling all over the world for rallies and speeches. They had a large entourage of followers known as "the troops," and they spent a significant amount of time in the company of these troops, many of whom were adoring women. When I was a teenager, I heard rumors that female members of this entourage were regularly throwing themselves at my father and uncle, and I finally decided that I needed to ask about it.

"Listen to me, Alveda," my father answered. "Your Mama is Mrs. A.D. King and will always be. Aunt Coretta is Mrs. M.L. King Jr., and nothing will ever change that. You get that kind of respect from a man, girl, and you'll never need anything else."

As the years went by I reread on numerous occasions the Bible passages about David, his sins, and his repentance. I reread, too, about the woman at the well and the woman caught in the act. I began to better understand the challenges that men and women face in trying to live godly lives. David's sincere prayer in Psalm 51 helped me to understand not only my own frailties, but that we can still be like David, people after God's own heart. Here are some verses from that psalm of repentance:

HAVE MERCY ON ME, O GOD,

according to your unfailing love;
according to your great compassion
blot out my transgressions.
Wash away all my iniquity and cleanse me from my sin.

For I know my transgressions,
and my sin is always before me.
Cleanse me with hyssop, and I will be clean;
wash me, and I will be whiter than snow.
Hide your face from my sins and blot out all my
  iniquity.
Create in me a pure heart, O God, and renew a
  steadfast spirit within me.
Do not cast me from your presence or take your Holy
  Spirit from me.
Restore to me the joy of your salvation
and grant me a willing spirit, to sustain me.
  (vv. 1–3, 7, 9–12 NIV)

I know without a doubt that my dad and my uncle loved the Lord with all their hearts. That is why I will never forget Daddy's love for me and his desire for me to seek love and respect in marriage. I have always taken his words to heart. Even though I fell short of Daddy's dream for me, I didn't fall away from God's grace. Today I have the courage to tell others that men and women who honor each other enough to stay true to their marriage vows forever present each other with the most wonderful of earthly gifts.

The Christian church has the best-kept secret around: Christians do it better! Any sex outside of God-ordained marriage is counterfeit and unfulfilling, and this is doubly true of sex that involves being unfaithful to your spouse. However, sensual love is celebrated within marriage. The marriage bed is undefiled (Heb. 13:4). Husbands and wives who allow themselves the full freedom of the sexual enjoyment God has granted them enjoy extraordinary levels of pleasure and satisfaction. Proverbs 5:19 talks about being intoxicated by sexual love.

The bottom line is love—the real love that everyone needs and everyone deserves. We owe it to ourselves to acknowledge and share the truth in love. Love never fails. Ungodly sex does, and if sex is outside the divine plan, it will fail to satisfy, it will fail to deliver, and it will lead to unnecessary sadness.

When I think about how we should talk to our children and to each other about sex and relationships, I always believe that it is so much easier to embrace human sexuality the Bible way and to reject everything else. I'm not saying it's easy; it involves self-denial. But there is also grace when we fall. And there is intense gratification when we do it God's way. That's what my family has always believed, and I am convinced that we will continue to believe this generations from now.

I'd like now to touch on the redefinition of marriage and family happening in our society. We live in a morally permissive and self-indulgent culture. In twenty-first-century America, we are well on the way to redefining homosexual unions as marriage. Yet statistics continue to demonstrate that the most successful model for raising children is in the monogamous marital relationship between one man and one woman.

Many would agree that the nature and purpose of human sexuality is procreation. After all, in one of His premier commandments, God said to Adam and Eve, the first husband-and-wife team, "Be fruitful, and multiply" (Gen. 1:28 KJV). God is the Author and Creator of the human family. His design is good. As the old saying goes, "If it ain't broke, don't fix it." *Amen.*

Our family has never endorsed homosexual marriage. Daddy King warned us not to judge, but to love everyone with the compassion of the Lord, and to set our moral values and standards and way of living according to the Bible. Likewise, my father and uncle were very firm on respecting the biblical model for marriage. During their day, even divorce was actively discouraged. I believe *I* was the first in our family to become a divorcée, much to the chagrin of my elders.

Uncle M.L. lost a high-ranking member of his

organizational team, Bayard Rustin, because Rustin was openly gay. Rustin was convinced that the homosexual agenda should be included in the civil rights struggle for desegregation. But Uncle M.L. clung to the Scripture and refused to acknowledge homosexuality as an issue that needed to be addressed on the public platform where the battle for skin color equity was being waged.

He had strong reasons for this because he was a man of God, and the Bible is clear on this topic. It teaches us in Mark 10:7 that "a man shall leave his father and mother; and shall cling to his wife." And Matthew 19:5 says, "For this reason a man shall leave his father and mother and be joined to his wife, and the two shall become one flesh" (NASB). By the Bible's definition marriage is a union between one man and one woman. Other forms of human sexuality, including adultery, fornication, and homosexuality, don't fit God's design.

What about people who say, "God made me gay so He must have wanted it that way"? Jesus said that some men do find themselves without sexual desire for women. According to Matthew 19:12, some men are made eunuchs by other people and some choose to become eunuchs for religious purposes. But others, He said, are born that way. I take that to mean born without a natural sexual desire for women. Today people often assume Jesus is talking about castration, but that's not what He said. Babies are not born castrated. So is Jesus endorsing homosexuality? I don't see how we can say that. Whether someone is born without natural sexual desires or whether he or she chooses such a state, the divine purpose of human sexuality does not line up with fornication, adultery, homosexuality, or sexual perversion.

This is indeed a hard situation, but God is not the author of confusion. He is not cruel or double minded. He would not design a life to be homosexual and then turn around and condemn that life to misery by commanding that homosexuality is undesirable and unacceptable. If someone is born with a propensity toward homosexuality, God has the same answer as for any sin, including heterosexual lust. Turn to Jesus. The Bible has multiple accounts of people who were born with various conditions and in various states of existence, only to meet Jesus and be healed or delivered from whatever was their concern. Truly, there isn't a human ever born into this life without having to contend with one issue or another along life's journey.

God wants people to be healthy and blessed. This is why He sent Jesus to set the record straight and to set the captives free of the problems we face. Misplaced emphasis on our human sexuality can prevent us from fulfilling our purpose in life. Someone once said to Jesus, "If you are willing, you can heal me." Jesus' response was, "I am willing. Be healed" (Luke 5:12–13 NLT).

This goes back to purpose. Why are we here, and how do we come to live our lives in the fullness of joy that we really desire? Dr. Myles Munroe says that if people do not understand the purpose for which something is designed or created, then they will abuse what they are trying to enjoy. When humans misuse sex, they generally do not experience the thing they most desire. Purpose is key, and we can discover our purpose in the will and Word of God.

In the King family the Bible is the highest standard for human conduct. This is why I think it is so important to look back at the values that guided my family. We have always understood that, beginning with ourselves, all human beings are imperfect, in need of liberty from sin, sickness, disease, and social ills. Agape love and forgiveness have always been the answer.

In his sermon "Rediscovering Lost Values," Uncle M.L. said, "The first principle of values that we need to rediscover is this: that all reality hinges on moral foundations. In other words, that this is a moral universe, and that there are moral laws of the universe just as abiding as the physical laws."

We must rediscover our lost values and discover how, in the twenty-first century, we can offer freedom, justice, and liberty to all, from natural conception to natural death. We must make a new commitment to this fight that affords human compassion, dignity, and agape love to all human beings while embracing a biblical worldview for life, love, marriage, and family.

RULE NO. 5

Defend Life

In 1966 Planned Parenthood presented Uncle M.L. with the Margaret Sanger Award, named in honor of "the woman who founded America's family planning movement." Margaret Sanger was also a racist and a significant figure in the eugenics movement, one of the ugliest social movements in our history. Neither of these things was widely known in the midsixties. Regardless, my uncle was wary about receiving the award from the moment he heard about it.

That hasn't prevented Planned Parenthood from continuing to trade on his name to this very day. In a statement released on January 17, 2011, Cecile Richards, president of the organization, said that his 1966 award was "in recognition of his excellence and leadership in furthering reproductive health and rights. Martin Luther King Jr. Day serves as a reminder of how much we have accomplished and how much we have yet to achieve."

There are several problems with this statement. The first is that when Planned Parenthood announced it was giving my uncle the award, it was for "his courageous resistance to bigotry and his lifelong dedication to the advancement of social justice and human dignity." Reproductive rights were not mentioned in relation to him anywhere in the announcement, though the award citation did say, "Dr. King has lent his eloquent voice to the cause of worldwide voluntary family planning."

The bigger problem is that this simply isn't true. In the Planned Parenthood lexicon, phrases like "reproductive health and rights" and "worldwide voluntary family planning" are code for abortion, which my uncle never advocated. I know this because I grew up with him and, more importantly, I grew up in the same values system that nurtured him and informs every word in this book.

One of my uncle's most oft-quoted proclamations comes from his 1958 book, *Stride Toward Freedom*: "The Negro cannot win . . . if he is willing to sell the future of his children for his personal and immediate comfort and safety." While he spoke this in a civil rights context, this is an irrefutably pro-life statement. What he's saying with these words is that we must never sacrifice future generations for the convenience of the mother and father. His strong conviction was that any decision that diminishes the future for the immediate gratification of the present is a decision that does irreparable harm to subsequent generations. Positions don't get to be much more pro-life than that.

In his "Letter from Birmingham Jail," Uncle M.L. underscores this sentiment by speaking out against "such ancient evils as infanticide," yet another clear indication that he never would have come out in favor of the institutionalized killing of unborn children. Uncle M.L. never took a public position as an advocate for artificial, invasive birth control methods. In his day married couples typically used the rhythm method, avoiding pregnancy by having intercourse when the woman isn't ovulating. Since Planned Parenthood doesn't teach natural family planning like this, I doubt they had it in mind when they championed my uncle as a voice for "worldwide voluntary family planning."

I'm convinced Uncle M.L. never believed in the platform of Planned Parenthood. He did not even go to receive the award. My Aunt Coretta received it in his stead, delivering a speech credited to my uncle but which sounds nothing like him, including several statements that in my opinion contradict foundations of his own philosophy.

Please keep in mind that this was seven years before *Roe v. Wade*; he couldn't possibly have known abortion would someday become legal and Planned Parenthood would become synonymous with abortion. I am absolutely sure that Uncle M.L. would be appalled to know Planned Parenthood is the leader in an industry that is responsible for more than 56 million abortions since the *Roe* ruling in 1973, according to the Guttmacher Institute—that's 1.4 million babies killed in utero every year for the last four decades. It's important to point out that one decade before *Roe*, my uncle delivered his historic "I Have a Dream" speech. His dream never included that number.

❦

There's another reason I'm convinced my uncle would have been a leading figure in the pro-life movement: he grew up in the King household, and the leaders in our household were unequivocal in their stance against abortion. I know this at the most essential possible level because I was very nearly a victim of abortion myself.

My mother, Naomi Barber, and my daddy had been courting for three years. For those unfamiliar with the concept, courtship is different from dating. In a courtship a man "comes a-calling" on a woman at her home, and they get to know each other in the presence of her family. If they do go out for fun, they go with a group of friends, and the man has the woman back at her home in time for curfew. This ritual leaves all the necessary room for romance, but none for the temptations that so often undermine the futures of young people.

By 1950 my mother was in twelfth grade, and my maternal grandmother, Big Mama Bessie, who was raising Naomi as a single mother, finally allowed her to go out on a date with Daddy, *alone*. She must have suspected what was going to happen. "Make sure he wears a rain hat," she said before Mama left the house.

"It's not raining," she replied. "Why does he need a rain hat?" She didn't know that was slang for condom. Whether the rain hat failed or was entirely absent that night, I was conceived during that date.

When Naomi realized she was pregnant, she

panicked. Daddy immediately said he wanted to marry her so they could give the baby a proper family, but Mama didn't think she was ready to have a baby. Maybe she could find a solution in a flyer distributed in her school by the Birth Control League (the precursor to Planned Parenthood). The flyer suggested that women are not brood mares—that they can and should take control over their destinies and reproductive lives. As advocates of Margaret Sanger's infamous Negro Project, the Birth Control League worked to keep birth rates down in black communities. It advocated "procedures for mysterious female ailments," which actually included visits to doctors' offices for secret D-and-C surgeries that scraped women's wombs bare.

Mama told my grandmother she wanted to get an abortion. Big Mama Bessie said no, that they should seek counsel from their pastor and A.D.'s father, Daddy King.

As soon as they told Granddaddy about my mother's dilemma and her intentions, my grandfather turned to my mother and said, "Neenie, that's not a lump of flesh in your belly. That's my granddaughter." Now keep in mind that we're talking about 1950, a time well before ultrasound could confirm the gender of a fetus. My mother had no idea whether the baby inside of her was a boy or a girl, but my grandfather knew with absolute conviction. He then explained that three years earlier, he'd had a dream that my mother had given birth to "a little girl with light skin and bright red hair" (there's Irish blood on the King side, so red hair shows up on occasion) and that "she would be a blessing to many."

Upon learning that my mother was pregnant, Daddy King was certain his vision was about to come true. And it did. When I was born, I looked exactly as he had dreamed. My father, by the way, was so convinced in the power of Daddy King's vision that as soon as he heard my mother was carrying a girl, he began to work on my name. Alveda is a combination of his first name and a variation on the word *vita*, which is the Latin word for *life*. He gave me the middle name Celeste after his grandmother, Jenny Celeste, and also because it suggested the word *celestial*, and he wanted "to get Alveda as close to heaven as I can."

While this story is indicative of my grandfather's incredible prophetic intuition, it is also a testament to the values he grew up with and passed along to future generations. Daddy King learned from his parents that life is sacred from the moment of conception and that you never willingly snuff it out. His wife, Alberta, shared the same family values and passed this value for the sanctity of life along to their children, imbuing Martin Luther King Jr. and his siblings with beliefs that simply never could have reconciled with a pro-abortion position.

❦

I got a personal glimpse of my grandfather's staunch opposition to abortion when he told me about his intervention with my mother. But there's some important backstory to give first.

As a young woman, shortly after I married, I gave birth to my first son. It came after my uncle's assassination and the suspicious death of my father. My son's birth was one of the few joyous events during a year of great sorrow. But three months after I gave birth, my body failed to resume its normal pre-pregnancy cycles.

I went to my doctor to see if anything was wrong. I wanted a pregnancy test, but the doctor examined me without the test and said, "You don't need another baby; let's see." Then, without asking about my wishes and without my permission, he proceeded to perform a painful examination that resulted in a gush of blood and tissue emanating from my womb. He explained that he had performed a local D-and-C. Having no understanding of medical procedures, I didn't realize at that point that he'd killed the baby inside me.

Of course, lack of knowledge did not prevent me from experiencing the effects of post-abortion trauma. My body was sore. I began to develop breast inflammation, depression, and weight problems. I was argumentative and difficult to be around, and my young husband didn't know what to do. We argued a great deal, and we finally divorced.

In 1973 we tried to reconcile, and I became pregnant again. My ex-husband absolutely did not want this baby and, because I was away from the support of my family and my church base, I gave in to his wishes. I became a client of Planned Parenthood. A doctor told me that what I had inside of me "wasn't a baby yet," and that the procedure to flush it out of my body would hurt no more than having a tooth removed. All of this happened shortly after *Roe v. Wade*. What I was about to do was completely legal, but that didn't prevent it from being a nightmare.

The next day I went to a clinic to terminate my pregnancy. My medical insurance paid for the abortion. As soon as I woke up, I knew that something was very wrong. I felt extremely ill, in a great deal of pain, and completely empty. I tried to talk to the doctor and nurses about it. "It will all go away in a few days," they assured me. "You will be fine."

They lied. It kept hurting, it didn't go away, and I wasn't fine. In the years after the abortion, I experienced an onslaught of medical and psychological problems. I had trouble bonding with my son. I suffered from eating disorders, depression, nightmares, sexual dysfunction, and a host of other issues. I felt angry about both abortions, but very guilty about the one I willingly chose to have, and this guilt made me physically and emotionally sick. I went through a miscarriage and cervical surgery as a result of the abortions and had problems with my mammary system as well.

By this point I was about as far from heaven as I could be. I was divorced, guilt-ridden, and a long way from my church and the foundations of my life. In the midst of this I got into another relationship and became pregnant. The same scenario my mother went through years ago was playing out again.

To add insult to my injuries, as haunted as I was by my last abortion, I was so misguided at that stage in my life that I believed that having another abortion was the only answer. I told the baby's father, a medical student, that I was planning to end yet another pregnancy and he stunned me with his response:

"I'm not going to help you with this, Alveda. That's forty-six chromosomes—twenty-three from you and twenty-three from me—and I want mine back alive."

I was stunned. *What was I supposed to do now?* Seeking counsel, I went to Daddy King. At this point I knew nothing about his earlier intervention with my mother that had saved my life—nor did he know that two of his great-grandchildren had already been torn from my womb. Regardless, what happened when I spoke to my grandfather changed my world forever.

"They are lying to you, girl," he said. "This is a baby, not a lump of flesh. No one is going to kill a great-grandchild of mine, Alveda. You're going to have this baby."

Daddy King was unequivocal, and his bluntness shocked me from a stupor I'd been walking around in for much of my young adult life. From that day on, after science and righteousness came together, I never considered aborting a child again. I began to see that abortion violates the civil rights of a person living in the womb of his or her mother. I began to realize that God is the Author of all life, and that abortion violates God's procreative plan for humanity.

I went on to have that baby and four others. I am now the mother of six living children. While I have had to face some painful consequences from ending two pregnancies—the most heartbreaking of which are the fearful expressions on my children's faces when they ask me if I ever considered aborting them—I know that my ordeal has given me the experience necessary to speak out against the systematic infanticide in this country today.

Even with my own children, I have had to stand guard against the scourge of abortion when they were challenged with unexpected pregnancies. I have reminded them that babies in the womb are people; that they are as helpless as slaves in the hands of their slave masters, as vulnerable as people who are aged or infirm, yet all are entitled to life and human dignity, from natural conception or fertilization until natural death.

Let me be very clear about something. I fully support the rights of women. As a woman (not to mention the daughter of a man who fought so diligently for the rights of all people), it would be absurd for me to feel any other way. Because of this, I also feel a woman has the right to choose what she does with her body— except when her body is inextricably connected to the body of another.

The baby inside a pregnant woman is not *her* body. That baby is a distinct human being who should have all the rights that we convey on people outside of the womb. The woman carrying that baby should have no more right to kill that child than she would have once the baby is born. Abortion is not a civil right. It is the abrogation of the civil rights of an innocent and entirely defenseless human being.

In the debate over abortion, the foremost civil right is the child's. Our Declaration of Independence states that we are endowed by our Creator with certain unalienable rights and that among these are life, liberty, and the pursuit of happiness. If we are to live out the true meaning of our nation's creed, how can we treat some people as though they are not actually people at all? Every baby scheduled for abortion is like a slave in the womb of his or her mother. The mother decides his or her fate and does so at will. In the ongoing travesty of the debate over whether abortion and infanticide should be condoned, a voice in the wilderness continues to cry out, "What about the children?"

"Today I have given you the choice between life and death, between blessings and curses," Moses told the children of Israel. "Now I call on heaven and earth to witness the choice you make. Oh, that you would choose

life, so that you and your descendants might live!"
(Deut. 30:19 NLT). God says through Moses, it is our
fundamental responsibility as humans on this planet to
nurture our children, and we cannot nurture them and
ensure the progress of future generations if we snuff
them out before they are born.

Such values require each of us to take an active
role in creating a culture of life. It's not enough to rail
against the evils of abortion, no matter how abhorrent
it seems to us. We need to make an active, concerted
effort to instill these virtues in our children *before* they
face the challenges that my mother and I faced when we
were younger.

This means helping them understand how life bless-
edly begins at the moment of conception. (I've often
thought we should celebrate our conception days rather
than our birthdays, though I realize the former is more
difficult to pinpoint.) It means showing them exactly
what happens to a baby during an abortion, including
showing them photographs Planned Parenthood never
wants them to see. It means making available the irreplaceable comforts of home, family, church, and faith at
all times, so our children never feel so abandoned that
they make horrible, life-denying decisions. It means celebrating the unparalleled joys of sexual purity, delayed

gratification, monogamous married sex, and procreative marriage.

It's all about education, following role models, and learning from the experience of others, even when that experience serves as a cautionary tale. Doing this creates an environment in which a culture of life can flourish.

No mission is more valuable than this.

RULE NO. 6

Fight for Justice

W e will not be satisfied until justice rolls down like waters and righteousness like a mighty stream," said Uncle M.L., in his famous "I Have a Dream" speech. It's a quote from the prophet Amos. Many of my uncle's messages to the world have become ageless and universal because they are often based upon the eternal and living Word of God.

Among the greatest of his memorable lines from that famous speech are these: "Freedom has always been an expensive thing. History is fit testimony to the fact that freedom is rarely gained without sacrifice and self-denial." Of all the values that our family has exemplified over the years, I think we represent this one most emphatically. The cost of freedom is indeed high.

At one level you could say much has changed from the days when my father and uncle fought for equality in such an unforgettable way. Their efforts and the efforts of others who struggled alongside them and after them have created avenues of opportunity that were once unpaved.

But for all that we have accomplished, there is still far too much oppression in America, far too many people whose opportunities are painfully limited, far too many circumstances in which those who aspire to contribute more to the world succumb to the devastation and degradations of the day-to-day. And as my uncle said, "Injustice anywhere is a threat to justice everywhere" (LETTER FROM A BIRMINGHAM JAIL).

One need only drive through any of our inner cities to see how this oppression manifests itself today. More than 46 million people in America are living below the poverty line, many of these in our nation's largest (and richest) metropolises, and the situation seems all but hopeless for far too many of them. Caught in a cycle of desperation, most believe they cannot escape. In some ways, the oppression these people face is more extreme than the oppression my father and uncle battled because they don't have great champions like my father and uncle on their side.

Tens of millions are living in or near poverty.

Meanwhile, as we saw in the previous chapter, there have been some 56 million babies aborted in the forty years since *Roe v. Wade*. I quoted the line from Uncle M.L.'s book, *Stride Toward Freedom*, in the previous chapter. "The Negro cannot win . . . if he is willing to sell the future of his children for his personal and immediate comfort and safety." One of the primary excuses for abortion is that it alleviates poverty; but if aborting babies eliminates poverty, why are so many people in bondage to poverty today? America is still searching for success, for victory, and yet we are not winning because we are still losing our vital resources—human beings. Too many children are being sacrificed on the altar of "immediate comfort and safety."

⚜

Daddy King was an activist from a very young age. Born to sharecroppers living under the yoke of the Jim Crow laws, he grew up listening to preachers preaching the gospel and urging their congregations to stand up against oppression. This influenced him greatly, something that ratcheted up to an entirely new level when he began to work under my great-grandfather A.D. Williams at the Ebenezer Baptist Church in Atlanta.

Daddy King witnessed horrible degradations visited

upon the black man, including a lynching, and he knew that things had to change, that the status quo was not only deeply unjust but also completely against the will of God. He had a fundamental belief that influenced his children and continues to influence his family today—that the teachings of the gospel forged the key to freedom for the black community. He understood that the Word of Christ was our path out of suffering.

When he took over as pastor of the church after my great-grandfather died, Daddy King amplified his message in word and deed. He became a major voice in the NAACP. He organized voter registration drives to make sure the African American voice was heard. He lobbied hard for better pay for teachers in black schools.

Granddaddy was a financial advisor to the members of his congregation. One of his favorite scriptures was from Psalm 37:25: "I have been young, and now am old, yet I have not seen the righteous forsaken or his children begging for bread" (ESV). He was a stockholder in the local black bank, and he encouraged everyone in the community to have a checking account, a savings account, and a life insurance policy, understanding that through financial responsibility the community would grow. "Always have something in your pocket," he told us, "and I don't mean lint."

Daddy King often loaned money to back new investments and businesses. He did everything he could to raise up our entire community, regularly writing job recommendations for parishioners and even speaking directly to employers on the behalf of those who came to him.

"The spirit of the Lord is upon me," he said from the pulpit, "because He hath anointed me to preach the gospel to the poor." He was quoting Jesus' first sermon in the Gospel of Luke. His sermons regularly addressed how we have to have "faith, hope, and love, and the compassion of God, for the prisoners, for the sick, for the elderly, for the widows, and for the children."

❧

It's easy to see how his life's work influenced his children, especially his sons. Uncle M.L. spoke numerous times about the noble example my grandfather had set. Daddy King laid the foundation for men like my uncle and father to move the conversation from a local stage to the national stage and then, ultimately, an international stage by filling them with the vision of a people who bowed to no one because of their race and who supported their community in every way possible.

Even before they became the voices of the civil rights movement, my uncle and father created empowerment programs for their parishioners within the church structure. They created numerous scholarship opportunities and spread the word that, in addition to living by Christ's example, education was the key to a better life.

Daddy promoted credit unions for his church members and often encouraged people to further their education and to seek opportunities to become entrepreneurs, and like his father, Daddy was often sought after to write letters of recommendation for students seeking entry into college, for people applying for jobs, and often for those seeking promotions and even political advancement. He was always eager to help.

Before Uncle M.L. was killed, Daddy was a happy and fulfilled man. He enjoyed life, loved people, and wanted to see people be happy and successful. Daddy encouraged me to discover what I would enjoy doing in life and then prepare to be good at it, through school and positive life experiences, so that I would enjoy working and creating opportunities for success. I have followed his advice all of my life.

When we stand as a community, when we make sure that we help everyone to help themselves, when we never forget where we came from and how much we owe our forebears, we cannot be held down arbitrarily. "Nobody can ride your back," said Daddy King, "unless you bend over and let him climb on."

I am sad to say, but I feel this sense of community is sorely lacking in the majority of our inner cities today. Upward mobility is a fundamental part of the American Dream, and it is always worth celebrating when self-made people rise up in society. However, what is not worth celebrating is something that has become the norm: successful people forsaking the communities that fostered them to move into more desirable neighborhoods.

Whenever inner city entrepreneurs decide to take their money uptown, they leave a hole in the community. This sends a message that the communities they grew up in are not worthy of them, that these communities are places from which they need to escape. This is deflating for the people left behind—the people who, in many cases, helped the successful entrepreneur succeed in the first place.

In the days of my forebears, days of dramatic growth in poor communities, successful people used their success to benefit the entire neighborhood. Back then the object wasn't escape; it was enhancing the pride of the entire community. It is only through this attitude that downtrodden areas can be uplifted and only through this approach of man helping his fellow man that true opportunity—as opposed to opportunism—can be created and nurtured and expanded.

Not only does staying in the community offer an inspiring example, but it also offers chances. In the days of my childhood—the fifties and sixties—inner city entrepreneurs were creating jobs and programs to help other people in the area get a shot at something better. These weren't handouts; these were real jobs with real responsibilities. Only those who committed to working hard got ahead, but they *did* get ahead because the opportunities existed.

৵

In the midst of all of the lessons and examples regarding success for life, the King family has been long guided by an even stronger theme. It comes from the Bible in the sixth chapter of Matthew's Gospel.

One thing we find there is an encouragement for faith that God will provide "our daily bread," but there are two particular passages I want to highlight. The first is on giving to the needy:

Beware of practicing your righteousness before other people in order to be seen by them, for then you will have no reward from your Father who is in heaven. Thus, when you give to the needy, sound no trumpet before you, as the hypocrites do in the synagogues and in the streets, that they may be praised by others. Truly, I say to you, they have received their reward. But when you give to the needy, do not let your left hand know what your right hand is doing, so that your giving may be in secret. And your Father who sees in secret will reward you. (vv. 1–4 ESV)

First off, notice that Jesus assumes we'll be helping those in need. "When you give to the needy," he says, not "if." A community governed by faith is moved to charity. We are supposed to offer of ourselves and not make a show of it.

We are also supposed to trust that God will provide our needs.

Therefore I tell you, do not be anxious about your life, what you will eat or what you will drink, nor about your body, what you will put on. Is not life more than food, and the body more than clothing?

Look at the birds of the air: they neither sow nor reap nor gather into barns, and yet your heavenly Father feeds them. Are you not of more value than they? And which of you by being anxious can add a single hour to his span of life? And why are you anxious about clothing? Consider the lilies of the field, how they grow: they neither toil nor spin, yet I tell you, even Solomon in all his glory was not arrayed like one of these. But if God so clothes the grass of the field, which today is alive and tomorrow is thrown into the oven, will he not much more clothe you, O you of little faith? Therefore do not be anxious, saying, "What shall we eat?" or "What shall we drink?" or "What shall we wear?" For the Gentiles seek after all these things, and your heavenly Father knows that you need them all. But seek first the kingdom of God and his righteousness, and all these things will be added to you. (vv. 25–33 ESV)

Because the men and women in my family before me understood and had the spiritual foundation found in these verses, they were able to be shining examples in their communities during their lifetimes.

I believe if they were alive today Daddy King, my father, and my uncle would all be rallying inner city businesspeople to be active, contributing, and *continuing* members of their communities. They would be exhorting these businesspeople not only to make jobs and opportunities but also to create ways for people to raise themselves up and sustain themselves at a level that fosters self-respect.

This is so much better than offering welfare. Welfare is nothing more than a Band-Aid, and not a particularly good Band-Aid at that. It might solve the immediate need of getting someone enough food to eat for a week, but it does nothing to help that person break out of the cycle of poverty.

This is not to suggest that government has no role in addressing this problem. It just has a decidedly different role than the one it is taking. What the government needs to do is create programs that allow everyone the opportunity to contribute to society, to feel the inner peace of doing something meaningful with their lives. Rather than welfare, what we need is an incentive program, gradated over a period of five years, to help families stand on their feet again.

First, we need to change the system so it doesn't penalize intact families. Right now it is far more profitable for welfare recipients to be single parents, and that is eroding the fabric of our society. Next, we need to set up a system in which we subsidize people while they are learning a trade or a profession, with the understanding that, over the course of five years, this subsidy will go down to nothing.

This accomplishes two enormously important things: it offers opportunity and it demands responsibility. Those who grasp the opportunity will do so knowing that only if they take responsibility to ultimately sustain themselves will they be able to thrive. I truly believe that the vast majority of people in our inner cities want this and will rise to the occasion.

◈

Perhaps the biggest roadblock we face in the effort to achieve justice is complacency. It is all too easy to convince ourselves that we have made sufficient progress, that our land is a more tolerant one, that people have greater access to opportunity than before.

Some of this is true. While it's impossible to measure, there certainly seems to be less outright racism in America now than there was when my father and uncle embarked on their mission. We're a long way from the days when the Reverend Billy Graham risked the ire of his following by reaching out to my uncle to help integrate his crusades. Meanwhile, the poverty rate has indeed dropped fairly substantially since the late fifties.

Still, the job is far from finished. Forty-six million people living below the poverty line is far, far too many. How can we ever consider the job to be done when so many people go to bed hungry every night?

My uncle spoke directly to the need for constant vigilance, even in the face of modest progress. In his Nobel lecture, "The Quest for Peace and Justice," given the day after the 1964 Nobel Peace Prize ceremony, he said,

> There is no deficit in human resources; the deficit is in human will. The well-off and the secure have too often become indifferent and oblivious to the poverty and deprivation in their midst. The poor in our countries have been shut out of our minds, and driven from the mainstream of our societies, because we have allowed them to become invisible. Just as nonviolence exposed the ugliness of racial injustice, so must the infection and sickness of poverty be exposed and healed—not only its symptoms but its basic causes. This, too, will be a fierce

struggle, but we must not be afraid to pursue the remedy no matter how formidable the task.

That was five decades ago, but his words have never been truer. Problems don't go away because you stop looking at them. The progress made in a place like Harlem—which is in the midst of an impressive revival with many local businesses prospering—doesn't offset the profound woes in too many of our inner cities and rural areas.

If we truly want the justice my family has always fought for, then we can never be satisfied that things are marginally better. We must always keep up the fight to do as much as we can to give everyone a fair shot at having a good life.

What this comes down to is rallying our resources. My uncle was absolutely right: we have no shortage of human resources. We only need to put them to the best possible use. For those of us who are living well, it means giving back to our communities, offering chances and guidance to those who are starving to contribute. For those who are struggling to rise out of difficult situations, it means committing to making the most of opportunities when they come your way, to never accepting your fate, to always believing that the best in you will be allowed to shine.

It is time for us to redouble our efforts to achieve a new level of justice. In that same lecture, my uncle said:

> Before we reach the majestic shores of the Promised Land, there is a frustrating and bewildering wilderness ahead. We must still face prodigious hilltops of opposition and gigantic mountains of resistance. But with patient and firm determination we will press on until every valley of despair is exalted to new peaks of hope, until every mountain of pride and irrationality is made low by the leveling process of humility and compassion; until the rough places of injustice are transformed into a smooth plane of equality of opportunity. (THE QUEST FOR PEACE AND JUSTICE)

He understood that this was an epic quest, a quest that extended from generation to generation. We need to remember the spirit of those words now and seek to bring a new level of mission to the drive for justice.

RULE NO. 7

Care for the Needy

As a guardian of the King family legacy, I have grown to realize there is a certain credo established in our bloodline, requiring us to serve God and the human family with a depth of spiritual commitment accompanied by the tenets of servant leadership and a commitment to upholding our ancestral/tribal family values, which are founded in faith in God and His agape love.

We can trace this legacy back for six generations to the aforementioned Willis Williams, the slave preacher, his wife, Lucretia, and an immigrant of the Irish Diaspora, Nathan King, and his wife, Melinde. These valiant souls are the founders of the Williams–King family legacy.

Jesus said, quoting the sixty-first chapter of Isaiah,

The Spirit of the Lord is upon me, because he hath anointed me to preach the gospel to the poor; he hath sent me to heal the brokenhearted, to preach deliverance to the captives, and recovering of sight to the blind, to set at liberty them that are bruised. (Luke 4:18 KJV)

In our family we care for the "least of these." We feed the hungry, clothe the sick, visit those in prison, and we do all that we can as servant leaders to serve God and minister to His people. Of course, from generation to generation our methods of ministry have varied, and yet we still care about the poor, the sick, the hungry, and the downtrodden.

❧

During his 1964 Nobel lecture, my uncle said, "I have the audacity to believe that peoples everywhere can have three meals a day for their bodies, education and culture for their minds, and dignity, equality, and freedom for their spirits."

A few years later he delivered a sermon called "Remaining Awake Through a Great Revolution" at the National Cathedral in Washington, D.C., and said,

The destiny of the United States is tied up with the destiny of India and every other nation . . . I started thinking of the fact that we spend in America millions of dollars a day to store surplus food, and I said to myself, "I know where we can store that food free of charge—in the wrinkled stomachs of millions of God's children all over the world who go to bed hungry at night."

In both of these proclamations, my uncle was speaking about values we have long held in the King family. Our inspiration comes from Jesus Christ. Jesus told us the poor will always be with us, but He also told us that it would be unkind and simply wrong to ignore their needs.

He implored us to care for the poor and hungry if we truly want to serve Him when He said, "I tell you the truth, whatever you did not do for one of the least of these, you did not do for me" (Matt. 25:45 NIV). What He's saying here is that we have an obligation, as God's servants, to give aid to those of us who have the least. Doing anything less is tantamount to denying God Himself.

Our family has always believed that no one (and especially no child) should have to suffer the lingering pain of going to bed hungry, and that those of us who are fortunate to have plenty must play a role in helping those in need. When I was growing up, there always seemed to be people from the church around the table with us sharing a meal because they had a hard time putting food on their own tables. Similarly, we gave out dozens and dozens of baskets of food or bags of clothing to people who could use the help. We didn't do this out of any sense of obligation. We did it out of a sense of love for our community.

My father held this lesson closer to his heart than many. He was possibly the most generous person I ever met. "A.D. would give you the last dime in his pocket if you need it," my mother would laugh and say. It was alien for him to see someone who needed something and not help—especially at Christmastime. I would often go shopping for Christmas presents with him, and he set an example that still resonates for me. He would always buy really nice presents for the family, and I knew that this brought him a great deal of happiness, but he seemed even happier when he was buying presents for people who might not otherwise have much under their trees.

We continue that tradition today. We tend at Christmas to give more gifts to others than we give among ourselves because our general attitude is that we are always blessed. We certainly give each other meaningful gifts, but it is not uncommon for us to give more to those who have a greater need than we do. Meanwhile, my ministry, King for America, does a great deal of charitable giving, especially around the holidays. While we do as much as we can, we also expand our reach by supporting the fund-raising efforts of agencies such as the Salvation Army, Hosea Feed the Hungry, and other local church and community organizations.

Taking care of the "least of these" has always been a mission so entrenched in our family that sometimes the message would have a humorous impact in our often serious journeys of life.

One such occasion was when I was a little girl. Big Mama was trying to get me to eat some Brussels sprouts. "Eat your vegetables, young lady," she said. "Children in Africa are starving and we cannot waste the good food the Lord blesses us with!"

As I choked down the bitter taste of those sprouts, I knew exactly what to do. I took the rest of the sprouts from my plate, wrapped them in my snowy linen napkin, and held them out to Big Mama.

"Well," I said, "you can send them these if they are really all that hungry."

Years later when my kids tried pulling the same stunt, I could still see the twinkle in Big Mama's eyes as the roles were reversed and I coaxed the little ones into eating the food that God had blessed to be on our table.

Another time, when my daughter Jennifer was a little girl, already aware of my charities and ministry endeavors, she came into the kitchen while I was cooking. There was a charitable marathon on TV encouraging people to adopt little children across the sea by sending money every month to feed them.

"Mommy," she came to me and said, tears in her eyes, "I think I just bought a baby."

I was puzzled, but when she dragged me to the TV I realized what had happened. She had scribbled down the number, gone into my home office, and called to support one of the children! It was a good chance to affirm her desire to care for those in need.

Perhaps one of the most poignant experiences of sharing with the least of these for me is when a group of teenagers appealed to King for America for assistance in organizing a Thanksgiving dinner in their transient community. They lived in an extended-stay compound near my Atlanta office. They didn't want to go to a feed-the-hungry dinner. They wanted food to cook in their own homes, and they wanted to be able to share the meal together in the apartment of one of the matronly women who looked after them when she could.

We arranged to get several turkeys and all the trimmings, and we even took a chef over to the apartment unit where they were cooking. He taught them how to slice, dice, and chop. I shared some of my cooking tips. They prepared a grand dinner, and we all prayed and thanked God for their meal and all His blessings.

I want to add this: my understanding of hunger is not a purely intellectual one. I experienced it firsthand after my second divorce. During my second marriage, I had been living in true affluence, complete with drivers and household staff. However, the split left me in a position where I was struggling financially. I had to learn how to make ends meet, and that was a very foreign experience for me because all through my life, I had never needed anything.

The challenges associated with this hit me especially hard when I walked into a grocery store. I had been accustomed to buying anything I wanted there, but I suddenly had to figure out how to feed my family with the meager amount of cash I had in my possession. This was painful to me for a couple of reasons. One was that I was a very prideful person at the time and I found it difficult to accept such trying circumstances. The other was that I was accustomed to helping out others; the idea of being a person in need did not sit comfortably with me.

Admitting that I needed help and accepting help from others was very difficult, and it took me some time to do, even though getting food on the table was becoming increasingly tough. In the midst of this a very kind gentleman and his wife heard what I was going through and bought me some groceries. That was the most humbling experience of my life, but it was also revelatory for me. I began to understand in a different way how it feels to need and to have to ask for and accept help from others. In the long run this challenge served me well. It stripped from me most of my false pride. Before then I had been great at giving, but not terribly good or terribly gracious at receiving. Now I can truly appreciate the generosity of others, and it has added new depth to the generosity I can bestow.

That time of crisis is long behind me now, but I will never forget it and never lose the lessons it taught me. Recently, my children and I have been helping several families. We've been sharing meals for one young woman because she's raising little children on her own and she doesn't have enough help from other sources.

I'm so happy to share with her because God continues to bless me and those I love.

⌇

"I have been young, and now am old," the Psalmist tells us, "yet have I not seen the righteous forsaken, nor his seed begging bread" (37:25 KJV). This was always one of Granddaddy's favorite scriptures. It has become a favorite of mine as well.

I am now old. That means that I have gray hair and wonderful grandchildren. People often marvel that I boldly proclaim my age and rejoice in growing old. But to me being old means enjoying a long life blessed by God. Granddaddy was a righteous man, and as a result I have never had to resort to begging for food on street corners. He and Big Mama and Daddy and Mama taught me to love and obey God and to honor my parents so that my life would be long and rewarding.

Luke 6:38 tells us, "Give, and you will receive. Your gift will return to you in full—pressed down, shaken together to make room for more, running over, and poured into your lap. The amount you give will determine the amount you get back" (NLT). Now I am sharing the lessons of my elders with those who are following along the path of life's journeys that I have trodden. It is better to give than to receive. This, of course, means tithes and it also means charity to the least of these. The cup never runs dry when you give to others.

You know the saying, "Give a man a fish, you feed him for a day. Teach him how to fish, and you feed him for a lifetime"? It's certainly true. In my lifetime I have seen this truth applied to my life and to the lives of many others. In the King family, with the grace and guidance of God, and with the love of Jesus in our hearts, we help people to fish: to fish for creativity, for purpose, for inspiration to accomplish their goals.

As they pursue and fulfill their dreams, they cease being the ones who need assistance and become those who are able to help others. We help people to depend on God, to grow in grace, and to pursue God's plan for their lives. In this way they become free from hunger, poverty, fear, and all those things that keep people from living abundant lives.

RULE NO. 8

Work for Peace

Perhaps the word most closely associated with the King name is *peace*. Our family has a long history of leading the charge against injustice and intolerance, but we have always done it through peaceful means. It is one of our fundamental beliefs that great and lasting change can only come when accomplished with peace in view, and we have lived that value for generation after generation.

Peace begins with a commitment against the use of violence of any sort, including bullying, verbal and physical abuse, and other forms of nonpeaceful engagement. We can only find peace when we learn to love each other as brothers and sisters. We must overcome barriers of deception. We must cross the bridge of enmity to find love and peace together.

In Uncle M.L.'s first book, *Stride Toward Freedom*, he presented the Six Principles of Nonviolence, which are indeed footprints on the path to peace. This template is every bit as valid today as it was then. I would like to expound upon each of those principles here.

Principle 1: Nonviolence is not passive, but requires courage.

One way people misunderstand nonviolence is confusing it with being meek or sheepish. Not so! Choosing to deal with conflict or to address social change without resorting to violence requires tremendous strength and courage—much, much more strength and courage than it does to strike out at your adversary. You must be willing, as my forebears discovered on multiple occasions, to absorb the blows of your opponents and oppressors while staying steadfast in the belief that reacting violently will only diminish your position and hinder your cause.

Imagine how much less sympathy there would have been for my father and uncle if they'd chosen to riot rather than march. We saw so many others attempt to address the civil rights struggle in this way, and they often accomplished nothing more than inflaming the conflict. Daddy and Uncle M.L. faced so many inciting incidents in their lives, but they knew that they had to stay strong enough to rise above this antagonism if they were going to accomplish their goals.

Principle 2: Nonviolence seeks reconciliation, not defeat of an adversary.

One of the reasons nonviolence succeeds where violence so often fails is the goals are very different. A violent response is often intended to strike down an opponent, which leads to more violence because your opponent won't go down without a battle or develops such bitterness toward you that a retaliatory attack is inevitable.

On the other hand, a nonviolent response seeks to reconcile your position with that of your opponent. The goal isn't to wipe your adversary off the face of the earth, but to find a way to seek common ground, to live harmoniously, and to create a better situation for yourself that your opponents can accept.

My clearest memories and understanding of nonviolence come from the time when our home was bombed. Despite what had happened, Daddy implored the people to love, forgive, and go home. It took extraordinary strength to take the high ground during this terrifying time, but it was unquestionably the right thing to do. Over the last two decades I have learned that what the Bible says is true: "A soft answer turns away wrath, but a harsh word stirs up anger" (Prov. 15:1 NKJV).

Principle 3: Nonviolent action is directed at eliminating evil, not destroying an evildoer.

This goes hand-in-hand with the previous principle. Again, it is about the objective. The goal in nonviolent conflict resolution is not to pound an oppressor into the ground. It's difficult to see how anything good can come of that in the long run. Instead, it is to find a way to eliminate the oppression itself.

When my family fought so hard for civil rights, the agenda wasn't to punish those who had unjustly limited the rights and freedoms of African Americans. Rather it was to effect the kind of change that invalidated this sort of treatment. As history shows, we could only accomplish this through nonviolence. The violent attempts made by others only served to polarize things even more.

More and more I understand that when we worship God, continue to walk in love, and refuse to argue and enter into strife, we win. People ask me things like,

"Did you hear that? Did you see that?" And the truth is I do see, hear, feel, touch, smell, and taste good and evil. This isn't something I perceive in my heart or experience with my senses, but how I react to what is uploaded or downloaded into my life. I can love or hate; I can live or die. I'm about the business of living and being loving toward others, not harming others with my words, deeds, or thoughts.

The Bible says we "overcome evil with good" (Rom. 12:21 ESV). Evil is dispelled by love and kindness. Darkness flees from light. There is strength in knowing this truth and effectively applying this truth in all things. Whenever potential for strife, indifference, and arguments come my way, I pray that I am fully armored in God's Word and am ready to hold my peace, so God can fight the battle for me. I don't always succeed, and I do live to regret hasty words and actions. It remains a learning process.

Principle 4: A willingness to accept suffering for the cause, if necessary, but never to inflict it.

We have already established why inflicting suffering is ineffective. It is also morally wrong, as one's agenda should never be to make others suffer, even if they have caused you tremendous pain. However, part of the process of nonviolence is acknowledging your adversary may not maintain the same moral standards. Making a commitment to nonviolence is likely to subject you to multiple instances of pain and suffering. This is why it takes so much courage to maintain the position. It is also why it is so effective, especially when attempting to sway public opinion. Ultimately, your adversary is exposed as being morally bankrupt, and the purity of your position becomes clear. This accomplishes overwhelmingly more than violence can accomplish.

This reminds me of a story my mother told me about my uncle. She'd gone to Montgomery to visit M.L. and Coretta just after their first baby, Yolanda, was born. One night Uncle M.L. had just been released from jail, and Mother was in the front room looking out the window when he came home. It was just after twilight, and the streetlight was shining in through the glass. Uncle M.L. went to the mantel in the living room. Mother thought he didn't realize she was there. He stood leaning against the mantel, pulling on his tie and shirt collar.

"Neenie," he said, "they choked me with my tie. They pulled so hard that I almost died. But I decided that the more they try to kill me, the more I'll love and forgive them." Mother was speechless as she watched her husband's brother standing there in the moonlight, armed with the strength to love his enemies.

Jesus preached, "Blessed are they that suffer persecution for justice's sake: for theirs is the kingdom of heaven" (Matt. 5:10 DRB). I think that's why Uncle M.L. often said, "Unearned suffering is redemptive" (SUFFERING AND FAITH).

I have always sought to understand the depths of this truth. Several years ago I cowrote and produced a play titled, *Why Must I Suffer?* Back then, I understood that our actions and decisions would have corresponding consequences, either positive or negative. I also understood that my elders were long-suffering warriors, and that their suffering sacrifices were beneficial to humanity because they were committed to the lordship of Jesus Christ, and were suffering on His behalf.

As a young woman, I was an observer and even an admirer of the courage of my elders. I truly didn't realize then that one day I would become an elder, and that my children and grandchildren would be looking to me for an example to follow. Today, as a warrior who suffers many blows as I labor to stand for truth and justice for everyone, I am finally beginning to understand that those who agree to suffer for the sake of justice and righteousness will be blessed by God.

Principle 5: A rejection of hatred, animosity, or violence of the spirit, as well as refusal to commit physical violence.

Directly related to a commitment to nonviolence is a commitment to a lack of hatred. I truly believe real peace is impossible if you harbor hatred in your soul. Hatred festers. It leaves you with the sense that you need to resolve things in dramatic, definitive ways that are often the precise opposite of what would lead to resolution (more on this below). Hatred leads to violence, so you must teach yourself not to hate. You can begin, like I did, by observing and patterning your life after those who have mastered the principle of loving their neighbors as they love themselves.

Of course I was blessed to have some very positive role models as my teachers and mentors. I saw my daddy, uncle, and granddaddy stand up to jeers, rants, billy clubs, bombs, jail, and all kinds of violence, and they always responded to their tormentors with love. Their actions didn't seem weak to me. In fact they seemed very strong. They were my heroes.

In turn I have learned to return hatred with love because, as 1 Corinthians 13:8 says, "Love never fails" (NIV). In my vocation as a global missionary for natural life, marriage, and family, I come up against much opposition. Often I am accused of being a bigot and worse. I take the taunts and threats in stride, always remembering my uncle M.L. saying we must "stride toward freedom." Added to that are the words of my Master: "Ye shall know the truth, and the truth shall make you free" (John 8:32 KJV). The truth is we must learn to be fearless in our pursuit of love, justice, and righteousness. As Amos 5:24 taught us, "[L]et justice roll down like waters, and righteousness like an ever-flowing stream" (ESV).

There is a connection between love and righteousness that's worth remembering. God, according to Psalm 33:5, "loves righteousness and justice; the earth is full of the steadfast love of the LORD" (ESV). They go together like melody and harmony.

Principle 6: Faith that justice will prevail.

A commitment to nonviolence is a commitment to the belief that good will always win out in the end. Violent solutions are often quick fixes that might shift things in your favor for a short period, but usually come with extreme repercussions that might make your situation worse than it originally was.

When you choose to live a nonviolent life, the results might be slower in coming, sometimes excruciatingly slow. There might be many times when it seems that they aren't going to come at all. Faith, then, is critical, because the key to allowing justice to prevail is to stay the course and know in your heart that things will turn out as they should.

My mentor, Senior Pastor Allen McNair of Believers' Bible Christian Church of Atlanta, often teaches that envy, hate, bitterness, and strife can make you physically ill and bring torment to your soul and grief to your spirit. He will often say, "Think about this: are you upset with someone? Forgive the person and see how quickly that headache or pain in your joints will go away." I first tried his recommendation years ago, and I immediately began to feel better in my spirit and body.

As I continue to follow the teachings of Christ and His disciples, including the modern-day Bible teachers I respect, I find more and more that only love can conquer hate. I find the truth of "love never fails." Whenever I find myself thinking violent or hateful thoughts toward another human being, I suffer the consequences. It really doesn't matter what my point of contention may be, or even who is right or who is wrong. If I allow that seed of strife to take root, I will be the one to suffer the most. So I have learned to choose love and nonviolence as a way of life.

I teach my children this same message, and they are following along as best they can. I have every confidence that God will bring them to that place where they can even love their enemies and do good to those who use them spitefully.

❦

As I write this, there is a great deal of heated conversation about America's gun culture in response to the unthinkable events that occurred in Newtown, Connecticut. Many people want to see much stronger gun control laws. These people might have the right intentions, but life has taught me that anger and hate are not constrained by taking away a weapon. The civil rights era proved that baseball bats, lead pipes, and ropes are lethal when in the hands of evil men. Terrorists have proven that fertilizer, nails, and airplanes kill more effectively than guns. The weapon is not the problem. The problem is inside the human being who wants to kill.

In the Garden of Gethsemane, as Jesus was being seized by Roman soldiers and officers of the Pharisees, Peter took his sword and cut off the ear of Malchus, a servant of the high priest. Jesus answered this violence by rebuking Peter and healing Malchus's ear.

Jesus didn't take away Peter's sword; He healed.

Today He still heals.

We will not end violence by trying to take away guns. We will not end violence by trying to demonize guns. We will not end violence because human beings are selfish, unloving, fearful, fallen creatures who will find ways to strike out against others. The problem is us. The answer is Him.

Christ's agape love—selfless love for others—is not only what stops violence; it's what builds relationships. It's what strengthens communities. It's what makes people who think they're different and alone realize we're the same and together.

Politics and legislation are good for solving problems, but not all problems. If our leaders really want to create a society where gun violence—and, for that matter, knife violence, bomb violence, and every other kind of violence—is reduced, if not eliminated, they will stop trying to remove God from every sphere of public influence. They should stop trying to hinder the expression and practice of faith and allow the one thing that will bring true healing: God's love.

❧

The Martin Luther King Jr. Center for Nonviolent Social Change, better known as the King Center, was founded by my aunt Coretta in 1968 to serve as both a monument to my uncle and to educate about Uncle M.L.'s life and inspire with his message. The King Center has developed a sequential process of nonviolent conflict resolution, and I'd like to walk you through each of the six steps to show the path that so effectively represents our approach to achieving peace.

Step 1: Information gathering and research to get the facts straight.

So often conflict emerges because people on one side fail to understand the objectives and motivations of the other side. There are numerous obvious cases of this in the Middle East, Asia, and Africa, not to mention several instances on our own shores built around hot-button issues. Sometimes the result of this failure to understand is explosive violence that lasts years, decades, or even millennia.

One of the first steps in achieving peace and positive social change is collecting as much unbiased information about a conflict as possible. This information allows for the kinds of breakthroughs that make reconciliation possible without bloodshed. Understanding your adversary has value on multiple levels. It not only makes you better prepared for dealing with your opponent, but it also gives you clear insight into his or her thinking, which might allow for the possibility of conciliation.

Now, as I have said earlier, I have been accused of being many things, including being hateful, judgmental, homophobic, hypocritical, fake, and only God knows what else. I hate to admit it, but early on in my Christian walk, I *was* some of these things. I was also a quick draw—quick to speak, quick to judge, and quick to become angry and accusatory. The school of hard knocks and a loving God delivered me from myself and taught me to love others as I love myself.

So now, before I write or say something that could be considered judgmental or hateful, I pray and do my research, and ask God to color my ink with His love and grace. I don't apologize for reading and believing the Bible and agreeing that the Bible is the perfect standard for abundant living. I do repent for my own sins, and ask God to forgive me.

Step 2: Education of adversaries and the public about the facts of the dispute.

This can be a considerable challenge at times. Often people on the other side of a conflict aren't interested in hearing the point of view of their enemies—especially if their objective is to address the conflict with violence.

However, it is often possible to make inroads and to allow the less fanatic among your adversaries to begin to see the other side of the story, and this can have a dramatically positive effect. While it can be very difficult to make a breakthrough of this sort with your adversaries, it is decidedly easier to do so with the rest of the public. In many cases convincing those not involved with the conflict to be sympathetic to your cause is the most effective way to tilt the battle in your direction without violence.

Much of my work centers on gathering accurate data, informing the public of both sides of critical issues, and then praying they will be able to discern truth and benefit from the discoveries. My participation in such film and print projects as *Maafa21, Blood Money, Life at all Costs,* and many others are evidence of the thoroughness and sincerity of the goal to provide truth for a public who deserves no less.

Step 3: Personal commitment to nonviolent attitudes and action.

There is no better way to lead than by example. Obviously effecting any sort of change on even a modest scale requires having a team of people on your side. If you model nonviolent behavior for that team, there's an extremely good chance they will follow your example, your personal commitment to nonviolence will become a group commitment, and this commitment will carry out into the world you're trying to change.

Step 4: Negotiation with adversaries in a spirit of goodwill to correct injustice.

This relates strongly to Principle 5 of Uncle M.L.'s Six Principles of Nonviolence. A negotiation in goodwill is one devoid of hatred for one's adversary. If the goal is simply vanquishing your enemy, there's an excellent chance you will either lose or be stuck in endless turmoil because your enemy is likely to fight back with everything he or she has. On the other hand, if the goal is correcting injustice and approaching the purveyors of that injustice in a spirit of goodwill, there's the very real chance that you can defuse the situation, make some inroads immediately, and take important steps on the way to a lasting peaceful resolution.

Step 5: Nonviolent direct action, such as marches, boycotts, mass demonstrations, picketing, sit-ins, and so on, to help persuade or compel adversaries to work toward dispute resolution.

You've all seen the footage of the civil rights marches

my father and uncle orchestrated. I'm sure you've also seen news coverage of demonstrations and other acts of peaceful resistance directed at social change. These forms of protest are extremely effective for two important reasons: (1) they raise mass awareness of a problem, and (2) no one gets hurt. Riots and other violent actions might grab headlines, but they rarely generate the kind of sympathy that leads to social change, because the protesters too often come across as criminals. However, the kinds of rallies that shine new light on a problem can change minds forever.

I was arrested in one of my first demonstrations in the 1960s, when I was just sixteen years old. In my recent history I have been involved in several peaceful demonstrations, including leading prayer vigils at abortion mills, and the pro-life freedom rides. I will always believe in the effectiveness of this sort of demonstration.

Step 6: Reconciliation of adversaries in a win-win outcome establishes a sense of community.

Finally, it's important to remember that just as violence is rarely a useful tool, shaming and humiliating your adversary is rarely effective in the long run. Lasting peace in any situation is forged on compromise. When both sides feel they have maintained their dignity and the core of their values while also accepting they have made critical concessions, there's the very real chance that the peace will be sustainable.

Nothing brings me greater joy than having former adversaries join me in prayer to God for revealing truth regarding issues of natural life, marriage, and family. As one who once believed in another agenda and who came to see the light, I rejoice in being used to bring truth to a hurt and dying world.

It's often said that society can't legislate morals, and that hearts can only be changed through a combination of education and religion. That's only partly true. While morality itself cannot be legislated, behavior can be. It may be true that the law cannot change the heart, but it can certainly restrain the heartless.

My uncle reached that conclusion fifty years ago and spoke about it during an address at Western Michigan University. "It may be true that the law cannot make a man love me but it can keep him from lynching me," he said, "and I think that is pretty important, also" (THE CASE FOR LIFE). There is a place for executive orders, for judicial decrees, and for civil rights legislation at both the state and federal levels. Until the human heart and soul become aligned with the love of God, there is a need for laws to regulate unruly behavior.

We have an obligation to protect the most vulnerable members of our society—from little babies in the womb to the sick and elderly. We need just laws to give a voice to those who cannot speak out for themselves. A heart that isn't centered in agape love will be able to rationalize behaviors that are often self-centered and have the potential to bring harm to others.

When I was a little girl, my toe once hurt so badly that I found some scissors and convinced myself that the toe had to be cut off. It is truly a very good thing that my mother rescued me from my own devices. She showed me that all of the pain was coming from a splinter and that the toe did not have to be removed. Of course I had a screaming fit when my mother took a sterilized needle to my toe.

Adults are prone to the same childish behavior at times. We might choose a harmful path for ourselves only to lash out at the very people who are trying the hardest to help. This is why human beings need so much help. It will take a godlike love to rescue America, the global community, and each and every individual on this planet—from ourselves. While we wait for the human hearts of the world to line up with truth and light, we'll need to rely on laws and legislation in the meantime.

PEACE

Tell you what about peace.

How about I give you a piece of my mind?

Never mind that there's never enough of your mind
to spare.

Who can afford to give such a piece away?

Now, peace of mind is something altogether
different.

As in war and peace.

People go to war to find peace. Does that make
sense?

Especially since there's a peace that passes all
understanding—

Which by the way is ours for the asking—

If only we agree to agape love one another.

Now that's a piece of the puzzle, isn't it?

Peace out.

RULE NO. 9

Build the Beloved Community

It's a fact of life that our family legacy is inextricably linked to the subject of race. There's a certain amount of irony that a family which has fought so hard to fulfill Uncle M.L.'s dream could be forever connected to the problem of people judging others by the color of their skin, rather than the content of their character.

There's a further irony here in that for generations our family has maintained the belief that, while the people of the world may come from a variety of ethnicities, they all come from one race—the human race. I remember Granddaddy saying on any number of occasions, "I'm a man just like any other man." His father was half Irish and lived the tenets of life as one race. We have always believed that, while cultural distinctions make us interesting, the vague genetic distinctions that come from the heritage of our forebears have no effect on who we are as people.

Most famously, though, is the message my uncle first brought to the world in the late fifties and then carried with him for the rest of his life. Uncle M.L. spoke of his vision for a "Beloved Community," one where "brotherhood is a reality." In a 1957 pamphlet outlining the mission of the newly formed Southern Christian Leadership Conference, he declared the "ultimate goal is genuine intergroup and interpersonal living—*integration.*"

He saw the world for what it truly is—a land populated by the human race and one that celebrated both our commonalities and our rich diversities. "This will require a qualitative change in our souls," he said, "as well as a quantitative change in our lives" (NON-VIOLENCE: THE ONLY ROAD TO FREEDOM). To him, this was both fundamental and inevitable. "We are tied together in the single garment of destiny, caught in an inescapable network of mutuality" (REMAINING AWAKE THROUGH A GREAT REVOLUTION).

Of course, this ideal of one race hardly began with my family. According to the book of Acts, God "made also of one blood every nation of men, to dwell upon all the face of the earth—having ordained times before appointed, and the bounds of their dwellings" (17:26 YLT). The message in the Bible is unmistakable: we all come from the same original ancestors. At the most fundamental level, we all share the same blood. We are all built the same way; we all feel love and joy and pain and desire for community. We all have hopes and we all have connections to other human beings. (Yes, I realize that there are exceptions to each of these cases, but the exceptions are so exceedingly rare that they do nothing to diminish the larger point.)

We have physical differences, of course. Our complexions vary; our hair has different textures; our eyes different shapes. Even our genes have subtle differences depending on our lineage. But these differences are akin to the differences in a field of wildflowers. When you look at that field, you don't see only blue flowers or yellow flowers. You see a vast palette of colors, and that rainbow is part of what brings us joy in admiring nature. Similarly, when we gaze upon a forest, we don't see row after row of the same trees with the same types of leaves, all of the same height. We see a variety of trees blended together, and when their leaves change in the fall, we marvel at the panoply of color.

There are differences, but there is one overriding commonality, one great unifier. "Man is a child of God," my uncle preached in his 1967 Christmas Eve sermon, "made in His image, and therefore must be respected as such . . . [W]hen we truly believe in the sacredness of human personality, we won't exploit people, we won't trample over people with the iron feet of oppression, we won't kill anybody."

⌇

I had very little awareness of racial bigotry when I was growing up, surprising as that might sound. I was raised in a close, nurturing community, and my family did as much as they could to insulate me from racism. We never ate at restaurants outside our neighborhood; no one told me at the time that this was because so many places wouldn't serve us. Grandmother always made me go to the bathroom at home before outings; she didn't want to explain the "white" and "colored" hanging over restroom doors.

I really didn't get a vivid firsthand picture of racism until I traveled with my father to Birmingham,

Alabama. As we drove through some of the wealthier—and exclusively white—neighborhoods, I asked him why we didn't live in a place that looked like this. After years of keeping me isolated, he began to explain to me why that was the case. Later when he went to Louisville to begin the Kentucky Christian Leadership Conference, I was right beside him during the open housing marches where we rallied for the right for all of us to live anywhere we could afford.

If that was the extent of my experience with racism, I would have been truly fortunate. But you already know that racism exacted a horrible toll on my family, and for a time I nearly succumbed to the hatred that allows racism to fester. Soon after Uncle M.L. was killed, I went away to college at Murray State. I had two roommates, Palmer, who was black, and Suzie, who was white. One day the subject of race came up, and the emotions I'd been harboring came to the surface. I wept. Suzie tried to comfort me, but I rejected her. What did she know about the feelings of black people? "Get away from me," I yelled. "I hate you—you killed my uncle!"

Those were the same feelings my father had been trying to get me to let go of since Uncle M.L. was killed. Yet I was still seething with contempt for the people who had stolen him from us. "I hate white people," I said to my father over and over again. "They killed my uncle."

Daddy was always an extremely loving and patient man, and he maintained that patience even in the face of devastating grief. He also maintained his belief in the Beloved Community. "White people didn't kill your uncle," he said to me. "That was the devil." He refused to allow me to hate, and he reminded me of his unfailing belief in our mutuality. That he was able to offer this example in the face of such an overwhelming tragedy at a time when he'd just lost the brother he loved so very much was a lesson I will never allow myself to forget. I'm just glad that Daddy didn't give up and that he kept teaching me to love and forgive until the day he died.

Not everybody in my family forgave the events of that dreadful day as easily. Years later Daddy King still carried an intense anger against some of the people who were with my uncle when he died. He held his greatest anger for Jesse Jackson, who had been with my uncle— trying to convince him in heated tones that nonviolence might no longer be the answer—when the shooting occurred. Daddy King believed it was Jackson's job to protect his son, and he wouldn't forgive Jackson for fail-ing in that duty.

This conflict was finally resolved at Jimmy Carter's presidential nomination at the 1976 Democratic Party Convention. By this point Daddy King was backstage in the wings resting in a wheelchair, and as he prepared to go on the platform with the soon-to-be President Carter, someone told him that Jesse Jackson wanted to speak with him. Granddaddy bitterly refused, claiming that Jackson was responsible for the death of his son.

Though I knew of his feelings for Jackson, I felt that I couldn't let this pass. "Granddaddy, I don't understand," I said. "I thought you always told me that we can't hate anybody. Doesn't that mean Jesse Jackson too?"

Granddaddy looked at me with pain and confusion in his eyes. Finally he nodded slowly and said, "You're right, girl." With that he told the man who'd come to tell him of Jackson's request that he would be willing to see him. What I witnessed then was one of the most touching moments I've experienced in my life, and one of the clearest indications of the power of love.

When Jesse Jackson came up to my grandfather, his face bore years of anguish and grief. He sat on Daddy King's lap, put his arms around his neck, and wailed, "I'm so sorry." Granddaddy was obviously moved by this declaration. "I forgive you," he said, and the two men at last got to mourn my uncle together. Everyone who witnessed it was changed by the event.

ᘐᕀ

As I write this, it has been more than thirty-seven years since that day at Jimmy Carter's nomination and subsequent election. In that time, much has changed, including the fact that a black man just completed his second presidential inauguration. Still, as much as we've accomplished, my uncle's vision of a Beloved Community remains in many ways unfulfilled.

The Beloved Community calls for us to fight against poverty, discrimination, and violence in every form. And as human history unfolds, the forms that discrimination and violence take will evolve and change. Yet our commitment to overcome them must not change, and we must not shrink from the work of justice, no matter how unpopular it may become or how satisfied some people might be with how far we've come. Beyond our borders, we need to stand with our brothers and sisters who are the victims of racial discrimination and so-called ethnic cleansing. As Americans, our message carries all over the world, and we must always raise our voices to cry out against injustice.

"We must all learn to live together as brothers," said Uncle M.L., and I'll add sisters here, "or we will all perish together as fools" (REMAINING AWAKE THROUGH A GREAT REVOLUTION). We must finally realize that we all come from the same source, and it is more essential than ever that we realize we are all united in our humanity. Once we the people of America and indeed the whole world admit and acknowledge our commonality, then oppression and bigotry can cease to exist in America and beyond.

RULE NO. 10

Find Your Joy

As an American, I was raised to believe that the pursuit of happiness is an inalienable right, an expression of life for everyone regardless of ethnicity, socioeconomic status, or other factors that distinguish one people group from another. Opinions vary on the nature of happiness, and one person's sugar is another's poison. "Justice is a joy to the godly," said Solomon, "but it terrifies evildoers" (Prov. 21:15 NLT).

As a member of the King family, I believe that every human being has a right that goes much deeper than the mere pursuit of happiness. On life's journey we should add to our pursuits the promise that comes with everlasting joy. Psalm 30:5 tells us that "weeping may endure for a night, but joy cometh in the morning" (KJV).

In my family we have experienced our share of weeping that endured through the night, and yet we always waited for the morning with anticipation of deliverance that comes from the joy of the Lord being our strength. We also always understood there's a profound difference between happiness and joy.

⌣

Happiness is a mercurial, fleeting expression subject to change with the shifting tides and the setting sun. But that's not true of joy. Joy is a deeper, more lasting experience subject to remain even as the tears flow and the cold winds blow.

Happiness is something that is very close to the surface. We can attain it from the simplest of things. For example, when I join my youngest grandchildren in the backyard to blow bubbles, the sound of their laughter makes me happy. Of course the euphoria quickly dissipates when I return to the chores in the house that can include cleaning up the sticky floors and fingerprints from the explorations of the little darlings when they come to visit.

On the other hand, when I consider how all of my grandchildren were allowed to be born and are growing into their destinies, our family reaching into the future generation by generation, I experience joy. "Children," says Psalm 127:3, "are a gift from the LORD" (NLT).

People often find happiness in acquiring and enjoying material goods, in television shows we like, in a nice meal at a friend's house, and other pleasurable experiences. But all these things pass.

I am a science fiction fan. One of my favorite stories is the *Star Trek* series—no matter which version, no matter what decade or century, I'm a Trekkie. Daddy and Uncle M.L. were fans as well. In fact Uncle M.L. encouraged Nichelle Nichols to keep her role as Uhura on the original series when Nichelle was feeling despondent over being marginalized. My favorite character has always been Mr. Spock, portrayed by Leonard Nimoy.

In the episode "Amok Time," Spock said something we would do well to remember: "After a time, you may find that having is not so pleasing a thing, after all, as wanting. It is not logical, but it is often true."

I mention this quote only because so many times in life, I have wanted a thing, believing it would make me happy. For instance, I always wanted a Jaguar. And then I finally had my chance. Someone offered me one at a very low price. I was thrilled—for a while. It was a vintage machine, but it was also very high maintenance.

I soon discovered that wanting the car was much more pleasurable than having to pay the cost of keeping it in top working condition.

Sure, we can gain happiness from experiencing good fortune or from getting something we desire. Happiness is a good thing—certainly much better than unhappiness—but it doesn't hold a candle to joy.

Joy comes from a richer place. I like to say that the fountain of joy is much deeper than the well of happiness. Joy comes from understanding that you are truly blessed and your blessings are not ephemeral things. Happiness comes and goes, but when you find joy—rich, abiding joy—it lasts for a very, very long time; joy can last forever.

I have experienced my share of joy over the years. Experiencing the birth of my children and my grandchildren and seeing them begin to fulfill their dreams has been a source of profound joy for me.

I have worked hard to accomplish certain goals, like writing books, composing songs, getting a business degree, winning a political seat, and gaining a presidential appointment. Some of these accomplishments were based upon my own dreams, and some were the visions of others.

Granddaddy, for example, always wanted a preacher, a businessman, and a politician in his family tree. Well, the preachers came early with Daddy and Uncle M.L. Aunt Christine first went to college to pursue an MBA, but racism and sexism derailed her plans. She was before her time—the world wasn't ready for blacks and women in the Ivy League business schools. But this was just a temporary setback. She responded to those challenges by changing her major to education and later revived her business acumen by helping her sister-in-law Coretta manage the King Center. I, too, wanted to give Granddaddy his businessman and politician, and my second husband encouraged me to pursue this dream. I succeeded in earning an M.A. in business and served two terms in the Georgia legislature.

Publishing songs and books were more instinctual desires for me, as was the desire to be an artist, among other creative ventures. By far my favorite vocation beyond being a mother and a grandmother remains my nineteen years as a college professor. I experience a great sense of joy when I meet my former students and hear their success stories. One, for instance, is a woman who became a mayor.

The effort I put into these pursuits and the sense of fulfillment I gained from making these goals reality has brought me a lasting sense of accomplishment. Real joy still remains in those because they were the product of great commitment and have helped in many ways to define who I am.

⌇

Overwhelmingly, though, the most joyful experience in my life came in 1983 when I accepted Jesus Christ as my personal Lord and Savior. Coming from a family of preachers, I knew practically from birth that Jesus was a savior, and I always believed He was born of the Virgin Mary, died on the cross, and rose again. I could read the Bible and find certain passages that I related to, though my relationship with the entirety of the Bible remained a casual one throughout my early adulthood.

Quite simply, it was not until 1983 that I realized that I, Alveda, was a sinner in need of the grace of the Lord. Once I was able to see this, and once I confessed it, the deepest joy I have ever felt came into my soul. This acceptance left me with the most intense sense of stability I have ever known. It began not to matter to me what was happening in the world around me because the joy of the Lord became my strength. From that day forward joy has been a constant companion.

This isn't to suggest that sometimes things don't get out of order. Just the other day, I had a flat tire. Who's got time for that? It wasn't joyous; it was a real pain in the neck. Still, even as I was going through the inconvenience of calling for roadside assistance and waiting for the tire to be replaced, I realized I was living in God's grace. On the bright side, the experience had a bonus; I let patience have her perfect work, and I counted the experience as joy because it was a trial that was overcome.

"We have experiences when the light of day vanishes," my uncle once preached,

> leaving us in some dark and desolate midnight, moments when our highest hopes are turned into shambles of despair or when we are the victims of some tragic injustice and some terrible exploitation. During such moments our spirits are almost overcome by gloom and despair, and we feel that there is no light anywhere. But ever and again, we look toward the east and discover that there is another light which shines even in the darkness, and the spear of frustration is transformed into a shaft of light. (OUR GOD IS ABLE)

This is the spirit of true joy and contentment that comes from giving yourself to God and from knowing that He will always take care of you. When you carry this inner joy with you, no despair can diminish it. Sorrows and tragedies will come, but you know without a moment's doubt that you will endure these trials and that joy will return triumphant.

I wake up in the morning knowing I don't have to worry about anything during the day because God is taking care of me. I have an inner knowing, an inner peace. I whisper a little prayer as soon as I open my eyes—"This is the day that the LORD has made; let us rejoice and be glad in it" (Ps. 118:24 ESV)—and I rise knowing God has my day; that, in fact, it is God's day and He's letting me walk in it.

I await all things in joy, anticipation, and patience. This is because of the joy of the Lord. God brings strength to me. He brought me to my mother and dad. He brought my children and grandchildren to me. God brings us every opportunity. Everywhere I look, I can find pockets of happiness and deep wellsprings of joy. I seek that out in everything in life. There's a joy in serving God that surpasses any other joy I can imagine.

As I said at the beginning of this chapter, I believe everyone has the right to possess true joy. How do you pursue joy in a way that brings you the great inner peace that I have come to know? I believe this is only possible when you remove uncertainty from your life and replace it with faith in God and His agape love.

Uncertainty is the enemy of joy. It creates conflict in your heart and mind that prevents joy from residing there. Faith, on the other hand, is the substance of things hoped for. And love never fails because God is love. Faith in that will lead you into that deep fountain of joy.

This is not something you can come to casually. You can't simply say, "Hey, I want to experience joy, so I'll buy into this whole God thing." Nothing this overwhelmingly wonderful comes without a significant commitment. We can only experience the joy and wonder of God's love after we lose ourselves and all that we consider dear. There's no halfway there. This is a lifelong journey. You either commit with all of your heart and soul, or you stand on the sidelines.

I certainly experienced some tests of my commitment after I was born again. When I was younger, outer beauty was very important to me, and I was especially fond of having nice clothes and lovely accessories. I would work with a seamstress to design very unusual and pretty garments, and I would dress these up further with gorgeous and often very expensive jewelry.

Not long after my born-again experience, I bought myself a beautiful bracelet. It was extremely unusual and it immediately became one of the favorites in my collection. I wore it with great pleasure; it provided me with a considerable amount of happiness.

One day I had the bracelet on and a woman I met told me how much she admired it and how gorgeous she thought it was. I immediately felt a surge of pride, but very soon thereafter I felt the Holy Spirit in my heart say, "Give it to her." I tried very hard not to hear this message. I loved that bracelet and I truly wanted to believe God was just playing with me. The message was insistent, though, and I came to realize that my commitment to my new way of life was being tested.

And so, cringing even as I did it, I gave the woman the bracelet. She was amazed that I was doing so, but she was more appreciative than I ever could have imagined. That was when I realized why God wanted me to give the bracelet away. It wasn't simply about ridding myself of the love of prideful possessions; it was also about learning to be more charitable. As the years have gone by, I have given away so many of my things, and it has become very easy for me to do. It isn't a sacrifice for me. In fact, it brings me great joy to give to others. Somehow the blessing of giving makes the joy of receiving all the sweeter.

I enjoy the things of the world, but I have come to realize that my greatest joy comes from God and from the peace I find in obeying God. That joy is truly irreplaceable, and I wish this joy for everyone.

If Uncle M.L.
Could Tweet

We need to remember that every age of every generation is the modern age. When we are born, there are things that humanity had either never seen or that had happened so long ago that we don't remember. That's why each new generation often thinks that the wisdom of the generations before is old-fashioned.

For instance, when I was born, television had only been invented a few years earlier. When my father, uncle, and aunt were born, automobiles were just a few decades old. When their grandparents were slaves, we all know how the way of their world was. Now, today, my children and grandchildren laugh when it takes forever for me to use technology they cut their teeth on. Yet while some things seem to change, some things never do. "History merely repeats itself," said Solomon. "It has all been done before. Nothing under the sun is truly new" (Eccl. 1:9 NLT).

In the early twenty-first century, social media is all the rage. I keep racking my brain for a way to communicate the message of the ages that my dear Uncle M.L. and indeed our whole Williams–King family have embraced: how faith, hope, love, and prayer are the keys that unlock the blessings of heaven. Suddenly, it came to me. *What if Uncle M.L. could tweet?*

So for all the Trekkies and all the tech-savvy brothers and sisters out there, this collection of quotes comes from the timeless messages and prayers of Uncle M.L. The sources for all of these tweets are listed in the Sources section in the back. I dedicate this collection to you as a way of drawing the themes of this book together.

❦

I'm just a symbol of a movement. I stand there
    because others helped me to stand there, forces
    of history projected me there.
We are made for the stars . . .

Let us join together in a great fellowship of love.

Heavenly Father, thank You for life, health, rewarding vocations, and peaceful living in this turbulent society.

God, teach us to use the gift of reason as a blessing, not a curse.

God, bring us visions that lift us from carnality and sin into the light of God's glory.

Agape love, repentance, forgiveness, prayer, faith: all are keys to resolving human issues.

God, deliver us from the sins of idleness and indifference.

Lord, teach me to unselfishly serve humanity.

Lord, order our steps and help us order our priorities, keeping You above idols and material possessions, and to rediscover lost values.

Lord Jesus, thank You for the peace that passes all understanding that helps us to cope with the tensions of modern living.

Creator of life, thank You for holy matrimony, the privilege You grant man and wife as parents to aid You in Your creative activity.

Dear Jesus, thank You for Your precious blood, shed for the remission of our sins. By Your stripes we are healed and set free!

Dear God, You bless us with vocations and money.

Help us to joyfully and obediently return tithes
and gifts to You to advance Your Kingdom.

Deliver us from self-centeredness and selfish egos.

Dear Heavenly Father, help us to rise to the place
where our faith in You, our dependency on You,
brings new meaning to our lives.

God, help us to believe we were created for that
which is noble and good; help us to live in the
light of Your great calling and destiny.

Lord, help me to accept my tools, however dull
they are; and then help me to do Your will with
those tools. [Paraphrased]

Our Father God, above all else save us from
succumbing to the tragic temptation of
becoming cynical.

God, let us win the struggle for dignity and
discipline, defeating the urge for retaliatory
violence, choosing that grace which redeems.

Remove all bitterness from my heart and give me
the strength and courage to face any disaster
that comes my way.

God, thank You for the creative insights of the
universe, for the saints and prophets of old, and
for our foreparents.

God, grant that people over the nation rise up, use

talents and finances that God has given them, lead the people to the promised land.

God, increase the persons of goodwill and moral sensitivity. Give us renewed confidence in nonviolence the way of love Christ taught.

We are made to live together.

Dear Heavenly Father, thank You for the ministering, warring, and worshipping angels You send to help keep and protect us in all our ways.

We are all one human race, destined for greatness. Let us live together in peace and love in a Beloved Community.

Have faith in God. God is Love. Love never fails.

It is our prayer that we may be children of light, the kind of people for whose coming and ministry the world is waiting. Amen.

AFTERWORD

No matter who the author or the audience, any discussion of values carries at least one big risk—the risk of *abstraction*. Values are not an abstraction, a concept, or a belief. To truly understand values, we must root our discussion in *the human person*, who is a concrete reality calling forth from us a concrete response. And the concrete human person takes his/her nature from the One God in Three Persons, Father, Son, and Holy Spirit, the ultimate model and source of unity, communion, and solidarity—indeed, the *Divine* Beloved Community.

Alveda King understands this. It has been a profound joy to know and work with her, and to know her family, for many years. As she fulfills her role as full-time director of African American Outreach with Priests for Life, I have experienced with her the joy of knowing yet another fulfillment of her uncle's dream that Catholics and Protestants would work together for the realization of justice.

Alveda approaches the themes in this book not merely from the perspective of *issues*, but from the perspective of *persons*. We don't just care about poverty; we care about *poor people*. We don't just talk about the values of family; we talk about *moms, dads,* and *children who need support*. We don't just talk about abortion; we draw attention to *real children in danger of being killed* and *real parents in need of alternatives*.

Alveda approaches human persons, and their real problems, with the twin convictions that (1) there is no such thing as a human being who is not a human person, and (2) that the only appropriate response to the human person is love.

It is love for the smallest persons and the defense of their right to life that has not only brought me and Alveda together, but which holds together the entire moral fabric of which she writes in this book. The right to life is not just one issue; it is at the heart of *every* issue, because issues matter only because *the lives of people* matter.

Few may know that in the time capsule that the King family placed underneath the new monument to Dr. Martin Luther King Jr. in Washington, D.C., is a statement, signed by Alveda and other family members, called "The Beloved Community and the Unborn," and it declares that in our day, the unfinished work of bringing about justice, equality, and nonviolence demands protection of the youngest, weakest members of society—the children in the womb. Only then can we be consistent in pursuing and protecting values—for they all hold together, and are indivisible, just as their source and origin, God Himself, is indivisible.

It is Alveda King's awareness of God, from whom every person and every value takes its origin, that shapes her convictions and inspires her actions. She is a woman of God, aware that when she speaks and writes of values, she is not putting herself above anyone, nor seeking to impose her will, but rather humbly acknowledging that because there is a God in heaven, none of us can be God on earth—and therefore the only path forward is one of absolute respect for the unity of the human family and the dignity of human life.

Father Frank Pavone

National Director

Priests for Life

Sources

UNCLE M.L.'S SPEECHES AND SERMONS

The Case for Life (18 December 1963)

A Christmas Sermon on Peace 24 (December 1967)

Conquering Self-Centeredness (11 August 1957)

The Drum Major Instinct (4 February 1968)

The Fellow Who Stayed at Home (October 1956)

I Have a Dream (28 August 1963)

Living under the Tensions of a Modern Life
(September 1956)

Love and Forgiveness (5 May 1964)

Mastering Our Evil Selves, Mastering Ourselves
(5 June 1949)

Nonviolence: The Only Road to Freedom (4 May
　　1966)

Notes for United Federation of Teachers Address
　　(14 March 1964)

Our God Is Able (1 January 1956)

Radio broadcast from Ebenezer Baptist Church
　　(summer 1953)

A Realistic Look at the Question of Progress in the
　　Area of Race Relations (10 April 1957)

Rediscovering Lost Values (February 1954)

Remaining Awake Through a Great Revolution (31
　　March 1968)

The Quest for Peace and Justice (11 December
　　1964)

The Three Dimensions of a Complete Life (April
　　1967)

Unfulfilled Hopes (5 April 1959)

When Peace Becomes Obnoxious (18 March 1956)

UNCLE M.L.'S WRITINGS

Advice for Living, *Ebony* (November 1957)

Advice for Living, *Ebony* (March 1958)

Advice for Living, *Ebony* (December 1958)

SOURCES

Letter from Birmingham Jail (16 April 1963)

The Negro Is Your Brother, *The Atlantic* (August 1963)

The Purpose of Education, Morehead College (1947)

Stride Toward Freedom (1958)

Suffering and Faith (27 April 1960)

This Is SCLC (1957)

Thou, Dear God (2012)

WEBSITES

The King Center (thekingcenter.org)

MLK Research and Education Institute (mlk-kpp01.stanford.edu)

Martin Luther King Jr. Online (mlkonline.net)

Acknowledgments

I always thank my God when I pray for you.

Philemon 1:4 NLT

To my natural family here on earth, I thank God that we share the legacy together.

To my BBCC church family, thanks for your prayers and support.

To Dr. Babs, Apostle Winston, Pastor John, and all the "believing" saints, "keep on believing." And to my PFL family, bless you! Lou, Joel, Peter, the Nelson Books team, it wouldn't have happened without you.

And to the entire Beloved Community, God bless you all!

About the Author

D r. Alveda King, a guardian of the King family legacy, is an ordained minister of the gospel of Jesus Christ and a grateful mother and grandmother.

She is a former college professor, author, mentor, stage and screen actress, and Georgia state legislator and presidential appointee. She has been honored and blessed to sit on several boards, and has received numerous awards and honors.

Through her ministry in her local church (Believers' Bible Christian Church in Atlanta, Georgia) and her vocation as director of African American Outreach with Priests for Life, she devotes her God-given gifts and talents of writing, singing, songwriting, producing and directing media projects, and other gifts to glorify God.

For More King Family Photos please visit the King Family Album at KingRulesBook.com.